Making
Experience
Work

Making Experience Work

THE GRID® APPROACH TO CRITIQUE

Robert R. Blake

Jane Srygley Mouton

McGraw-Hill Book Company

New York   St. Louis   San Francisco   Auckland   Bogotá
Düsseldorf   Johannesburg   London   Madrid
Mexico   Montreal   New Delhi   Panama
Paris   São Paulo   Singapore
Sydney   Tokyo   Toronto

Library of Congress Cataloging in Publication Data

Blake, Robert Rogers, date.
  Making experience work.

  Includes bibliographical references and index.
  1. Problem solving. I. Mouton, Jane Srygley,
joint author. II. Title.
HD30.29.B55   658.4'03   77-13002
ISBN 0-07-005675-7

1234567890   MUBP   7654321098

The editors for this book were W. Hodson Mogan and Tobia L. Worth,
the designer was Naomi Auerbach, and the production supervisor
was Teresa F. Leaden. It was set in Palatino
by The Fuller Organization.

Printed by The Murray Printing Company and bound by The Book Press.

Contents

43

Preface

The foundation of any human relationship lies in the way people deal with each other in solving problems together. This book is for anyone who wishes to learn to solve problems better: in the factory, at school and college, in the office, or in the home. It describes and evaluates various ways that can be used to eliminate the drag that comes from failure or partial success. Learning from problem-solving experiences also can reinforce effectiveness by making clear whatever in an experience resulted in success.

A basic observation is that sound performance, though universally desired, is rarely reached. Problem-solving methods to improve performance are the missing link. Why have Western societies been so long in discovering and harnessing these powerful tools of change?

The English-speaking, Judeo-Christian world is built on and continues to reflect, to a very substantial degree, the evolution of thought and institutions of Great Britain. The philosophies of Locke, Berkeley, and Hume emphasized the importance of individualism and freedom and of a rational problem-solving view of life based on logic and introspection. Add to this the parliamentary tradition which emphasized decisions based on polarization of majority/minority thinking, and you will see that both drew attention toward important aspects of the human situation, but each failed to regard some of the most critical conditions for problem solving, growth, and change. For example, *Robert's Rules of Order* provide a set of procedures for collaborative decision making, but there is nothing in *Robert's Rules* that challenges participants before, during, or after the process of decision making to critique the problem-solving effectiveness of the conclusions reached. The same is true in the U.S. Congress and widely through American industry. The committee structure of American universities is a shambles because they too have failed to recognize the contribution that improved problem-solving methods could have made for strengthening decision making.

The failure to recognize how a "silent," unstudied culture can mold character, dictate relationships, and control the direction of problem-solving efforts, often in ways adverse to sound performance, and the inability of individuals and society to exploit the powerful potential for cultural change and development constitute two continuing barriers which societies must learn to grapple with if anything like an emergence from the current period of ever-accumulating and unresolved problems is to be realized.

Reflecting on the above, not too much of what has been said is new. Certainly neither point of emphasis is novel. What may be significant, what is important, at least to us, is that we now know with reasonable certainty that these are dominant problems throughout the Western world. Further development awaits the application of more powerful learning mechanisms for focusing such issues. Offering critique strategies through which greater skill in performance and problem analysis, problem solving, and change may become available to wider segments of the Western populations is a next important step.

David Lloyd-Thomas, who is Managing-Director of Scientific Methods (Australia), took a significant hand in this project, *critiquing* both to revise and to edit the original writing into a more readable and useful text. Ms. Helen Inglis, also of Scientific Methods (Australia), assisted in this project. Our appreciation is expressed to both of them, and to Ms. Artie Stockton, of Scientific Methods, Inc., who monitored the project from beginning to end.

Robert R. Blake
Jane Srygley Mouton

MAKING EXPERIENCE WORK
The Grid Approach to Critique

Years of research and experience with Grid concepts lead to the conclusion that there are three concepts inherent in good management. One is the notion of participation. The second involves setting goals. The third is the use of critique to learn from work experience.

This book is about how to learn from work experience, and critique is the technical word for it. The term is often confused with criticism, but critique is the application of study and diagnosis to any situation in order to analyze that situation, how to change it, and how to generalize what is learned so that similar situations arising in the future can be dealt with in a similar, more efficient or more effective way. The other key issues in the Grid approach are dealt with elsewhere.

ONE

Learning from Experience

"In the final analysis," we are told, "experience is the best teacher." Yet many of us do not recognize the learning opportunities in the problems we face day in and day out. To a limited extent, this is because we believe there is little to be learned from some of our activities. It may be, however, that the problems we confront are rich with learning opportunities, but because we don't know *how to learn from them,* we gain little of the understanding that is available.

In almost direct contrast to these lost opportunities for learning from experience, we do know something about how to learn from textbooks. Accumulated, codified knowledge of the kind found in textbooks, in TV documentaries, in technical films, and on educational radio is of vast importance. It surrounds us—from an early age into adulthood. As students, we come to accept, probably incorrectly, that codified knowledge is more important than learning from experience how to deal with problems because we can learn in a few years some of the wisdom and knowledge that has been accumulated over centuries. As a result, we are conditioned to absorb classroom knowledge without ever finding out that we can learn from our own direct experiences, with principles of problem solving. Thus, the importance of learning from experience has become greatly underestimated.

What, then, are the formal ways of approaching problems from a direct learning point of view? First, there are scientific experiments, which provide a way of learning by solving problems in highly controlled environments. This makes it possible to determine what makes things happen in a particular way in one situation and quite differently in another. Though restricted in its practical usefulness because of its demands for rigorous control and conditions, the scientific method is probably the best problem-solving theory available today.

A second example is the evaluation of testimony in a courtroom. Here judicial procedures are used to reconstruct details of the actual experience because the inquiry is undertaken on an after-the-fact basis. The use of these legal procedures cannot be controlled in the same way scientific experimentation is controlled. Even though the rules of admissible evidence are very precise, findings are more subject to error and different interpretations than those resulting from the more rigorous, objective scientific experiment.

Both scientific method and judicial procedures, nevertheless, are formal approaches. Each is useful under specific conditions. Neither, however, is practical as a model for learning from direct experiences that unfold in our work, home, recreation, and social and other activities on a day-by-day, hour-by-hour, even moment-by-moment basis.

The question, then, is, what can we do under everyday conditions to learn how to solve problems in a better way? The way most of us go about learning from experience is very different from that of scientific method and judicial procedures. It is relied on, possibly to an excessive degree, and is best described as trial-and-error problem solving.

Problem solving by trial and error is just about what it says. Try something and if you succeed, all well and good. Repeat the same action the next time you encounter the same dilemma. You've *learned* what works. If you fail, try something else next time. At least you have learned something—you've learned what won't solve the problem. To repeat the same false solution when it does not work is like banging your head against a brick wall. It certainly does not let you learn what will work—and why.

Trial and error is mechanical. It is too unseeing to provide learning at the rate needed in a modern, complex society. It may explain how a rat negotiates a maze to get food, or how youngsters learn something before they can really analyze an issue and apply problem-solving methods to it, and how many adults respond automatically to situations. Yet, it suffers serious weaknesses at points in the sequence, one of which is the absence of deliberate thinking, analysis, and planning that often can precede actions as a basis for ensuring that the actions, when taken, will be sound. Without such planning, the actions taken may be far less fitting to the real requirements than they otherwise could be.

What options are there, then, beyond trial and error learning if we want to acquire more understanding from experience than we have in the past? *Critique* is a term we can apply to learning directly from experience. Critique involves evaluating action in a thoughtful way before the action is taken, during the action, or when it has been completed. It is important because the test of planning is in the results achieved and their explanations which critique establishes. Better understanding of the cause-and-effect actions that result in solving a given problem through critique is thus the key to better planning for improved results in meeting similar problems in the future. This may be why critique learning is now being recognized as a way to approach solutions of the range and variety of problems facing us.

A description of how critique was employed to solve problems encountered and thus to reach victory in a world sailing competition is provided by Edward Heath, former Prime Minister of Great Britain. He took up sailing when he turned 50 years of age. A few years later, just before he became Prime Minister, he captained the six-man crew of *Morning Cloud* to victory in one of the world's three top competitions: the Sydney-Hobart race.

Sailing is a particularly good laboratory for evaluating the potential of critique for problem solving. The variables that influence the success of one boat versus another are more or less balanced out or are under the control of the crew. How Heath did this is told in *Sailing,* and summed up below.

> On *Morning Cloud* we have tried as far as possible to do everything together as a crew. This begins with the discussions on the design and layout of the boat: it continues with an expression of views about

new members of the crew. We have our own kit, in part for safety reasons, in part because it makes for unity. When away from home we dislike being broken up; we prefer to stay in the same place. After every race we like to be able to analyse it together—to try to learn from our mistakes—on the boat on its moorings if we cannot get together on shore. It is the constant exchange of views and information which binds a crew together and enables each of its members to act in the almost instinctive knowledge of what the others will do in any given situation. Of course this is an ideal, but it is worth taking time and trouble over.[1]

Once the goal of victory had been established, achieving it rested on maximum use of human resources to solve problems that would cause failure if solutions were not found. Critique-oriented planning, based on full participation, brought forth the best understanding of what was to be accomplished, how members would coordinate efforts with one another and deal with emergencies, and so on. Critiques after the journeys were over identified weaknesses and strengths in performance needing correction or strengthening to gain the greatest possible improvement in performance for the next event. Though far more complex, Heath believes that successfully leading a company or a nation relies, in principle, on the same skills of critique to strengthen problem analysis and resolution and to identify and rectify weaknesses in the implementation of identified solutions.

Structure of Work

"How is problem solving undertaken?" "Where do we begin?" These are questions needing answers, and the possibilities for using various solution-seeking methods are so vast that at first it seems impossible to bring order or system into studying them. Yet, without some basis for seeing order and coherence, we are left only with the alternative that each episode must be examined in isolation, one after another, to find out what can be learned about problem solving in general. Repeated, episode by episode, the sheer magnitude of this task is so staggering as to be unproductive. Therefore, a model has been developed to bring the different varie-

[1]Edward Heath, *Sailing* (London: Sidgwick and Jackson, Ltd., 1975).

ties of work into a meaningful framework—to compare and contrast one with another, to weigh and evaluate similarities and differences. Generalizations which establish the basic principles, strategies, and techniques for critiquing any situation then become possible.

Since the structure of work varies throughout this wide spectrum, it is evident that one method of critique may be more suitable for learning from one work structure than from another. This does not rule out the possibility that any critique method may be applied to more than one work structure, but it suggests that one critique approach may produce better results than another.

How different activities relate to the structure of work is summarized in Table 1 and discussed in the sections that follow.

Think of a continuum. At one end is one kind of work; at the other, work of a very different character. Gradations along the continuum contain elements of both poles but in different degrees. The scale of the continuum relates to repetitiveness in the work. The left end is nonrepetitive; the right end, highly repetitive.

Discrete project work

At the left side of the continuum in the table, the work project is experienced as a "package." It is complete, a unit, with a definite beginning and end. No two packages are alike and any two of these discrete units are more or less independent of one another. A project such as signing a new contract is an example. One project may follow another but each is a separate and distinctive activity. It has a character of its own and the handling of one project in the past does not dictate or even guide the approach desirable to handle one in the future. Organizations that use project management, carry out contract work, or use task forces provide many examples of discrete project work. The same is true for organizations concerned with pure and applied research. Examples of discrete project work are provided in the table.

However, project management may itself develop traditions, precedents, and past practices which become "formulas" that are applied more or less mechanically to future projects. When this happens, discrete project management has become cyclical in character.

TABLE 1 Structure of Work

Organized activity	Discrete projects	Recurring activity cycles	Continuous flow
How is the work structured?	Definite clear beginning, intermediate activities, and an end.	Cycles of activity are repeated without major change in structure, yet each cycle has a new beginning, intermediate phases, and an end, and each is patterned after the previous one.	No beginning and no end, but a level of more or less steady and repetitive performance; a quasi-stationary equilibrium.
What are some examples?	New plant start-up; contracting with a supplier for major office purchases; installing a computerized MIS system; an inexperienced salesperson making a cold call; entering a diversification program by buying another company; government contracts; designing and launching a new product where no formula can be applied; writing a book.	Launching an advertising program where a formula is applied; developing a yearly budget; an experienced salesperson making a cold call; preparing a technical product manual from a preestablished outline of contents; weekly staff meetings; quarterly and annual reports; updating policy manuals; filing income tax and other government reports.	Assembly line and other fixed input-output streams; receiving and filling orders in a mail order house; billing customers for purchases; implementing contracts with suppliers for routine purchases; rate of telephone calls through a company's switchboard; company filing system.

SOURCE: From *Seminar on Strategies of Critique* Materials. Copyright © Scientific Methods, Inc., 1977.

Activity cycles

A second kind of work is shown in the middle of the continuum. Work structured in this way tends to be cyclical in character. A sequence repeats its main features, within specific time periods or specifiable settings. Cycles may follow one another almost without a break to define the end of one and the beginning of the next, making the work structure look like a constant flow. Alternatively, each cycle may be quite distinct, like a one-time-only project. An activity cycle is neither of these; it is in between both.

The model year changeover in the automobile industry is a shift-over from one activity cycle to another. When this happens, new designs are introduced and some plants shut down for retooling. In spite of this break between cycles, however, next year's popular-priced car looks—and is—distinctly related in style and perform-ance to last year's popular-priced car. Thus, there are predictable connections between a previous, present, and future activity cycle. Farming contains many examples of activity cycles of planting, cultivating, and harvesting, with the same or similar crop(s) planted year after year, cultivated with more or less the same equipment and manpower, and brought to market in essentially the same way. Each year is a new beginning, yet the previous year influences the one that follows it.

The same cyclical character is true for a number of different examples of individual effort.[2] A business or government executive arrives at work each day at about the same time. Though obviously different, the meetings attended are almost always identical, with about the same people, week after week, with minor variations in agenda topics. The boss gets angry in a similar way and to more or less the same degree whenever problems of one or another particu-lar category crop up, which are often the same or similar kinds of problems repeatedly occurring. A corporate management group might perennially be unable to finish its meeting agendas, even though the session time is increased. In the broader corporate set-ting, this year's annual report is different from last year's, yet often very similar in its main features. A few old problems were solved, a few new ones came into view. A few obsolete products were discon-

[2]Robert R. Blake and Jane Srygley Mouton, *Consultation* (Reading, Mass.: Ad-dison-Wesley, 1976).

tinued and new ones introduced to replace them, but the major themes recycle from one period to another.

An example in everyday life is an alcoholic who might start each day with a drink. The first drink is not necessarily at exactly the same time every day and the alcoholic may depart from a set pattern, occasionally skipping a day or two. But such deviations are variations on a recurring theme. The same holds true with smoking: the smoker consumes, say, one or two packs per day on the average, even though there may be temporary intermissions and up and down drifts. Likewise, the heroin addict may shoot up daily, except to forgo a fix when temporarily out of funds.

Learning about solving problems that have a cyclical character, therefore, can help a person, a group, an organization, or even a larger social system to identify and to break out of cycles that are less productive than they should or could be. Critique to bring about changes aimed at cycle breaking is useful for altering work that has this character.

A key factor is to learn how the past, as evidenced in traditions, precedents, and past practices, continues to influence the goal setting (or the lack of it) in the next cycle, and what to do to prevent these influences from perpetuating themselves.

Continuous flow

Work experienced as a flow goes on in a more or less continuous way, day in and day out, at a more or less constant rate. This is shown on the right-hand side of the table. Any continuous activity can be conceived as having a dimension of volume or frequency that can be plotted against time. Filling 500 bottles per minute is a rate. An average of 100 pounds of waste a day in a leather factory is volume per production run. An average of 25 rejects per 1000 units produced is a rate. Though results may fluctuate, all these indicators may be and usually are more or less steady over time.

The rate of flow may vary, as does traffic over the George Washington bridge, as a function of time of day. The rate is similar at 10:00 a.m. five days a week and at 2:00 p.m. or 7:00 p.m. However, this type of structure should still be regarded as a constant flow rather than an activity cycle that starts at one time of day and then ends, to be repeated tomorrow. Assembly line production is an example. Refinery throughput is another. Servicing customers in a supermarket is a third.

Once started, the activity has no real beginning and no real end; it is continuous. The second day picks up about where the first day left off. The level of results obtained may be retarded or advanced, but to stop to fix things is to disrupt the entire system.

Conceived in this manner, it becomes evident that many management problems involve learning how to increase or reduce volume or frequency over time from some previously steady level. To shift a rate from one level to another is a way of talking about increasing or decreasing productivity: currently the rate is at one level and the goal is to change the rate to a higher or lower level. Critique is a tool for learning how to bring about the change.

Combinations and permutations

Shifts may also be brought about in the basic character of the work structure for producing the same thing. Automobile production in some settings is currently being shifted from a *constant flow* assembly line to a team approach activity cycle type of structure. In the latter case, several employees are responsible for the production of one car, from start to finish, whereas in the former, each position along the line exerts its specific effort in the same way each time a partially assembled automobile is advanced up the line.

A scheduled commercial flight from New York to Los Angeles may be regarded as a recurring activity cycle. Each departure is a definite beginning, has intermediate phases, and a clear end, and these vary with weather, traffic, and so on. However, a midair collision turns a routine flight into a discrete project, and the form of critique shifts accordingly. A board of inquiry seeks to establish cause, and once done, to formulate new standards of flight operations, maintenance, and whatever might be necessary to avoid future mishaps.

Approaches to Critique

There are many approaches for learning to solve problems; there is no single best way. Our task, thus, is to study and understand the range and variety of critique techniques that are available and, progressively, to identify those instances where one form of critique is likely to be better than another.

The view that experience is an important source for learning to solve problems goes back into antiquity. Socrates said, "The unexamined life is not worth living." Aristotle maintained, "What we have to learn we learn by doing." A well-known advocate of critique in modern times is the Scottish poet Robert Burns, who said, "O wad some Pow'r the giftie gie us to see oursels as others see us."

The theoretical physicist Norbert Wiener introduced the concept of "steering" a mechanical or electrical system by using feedback loops.[3] The feedback loop has become so much a part of modern life that it is accepted without attracting particular attention. For example, setting an air conditioning thermostat at a given temperature and then connecting it to a compressor results in power-on and power-off actions as room temperature departs from the designated settings. A constant temperature environment based on feedback has been created. Any system that changes its action as a result of receiving information from its environment is a single-loop feedback system. Emphasis was placed on feedback as a learning mechanism by Ross Ashby,[4] who showed that organisms not only react to their environment, that is, single loop, but also shift their own activity to the environment by changing the environment. Kurt Lewin[5] understood the implications of feedback systems, not only for the control of physical or electrical systems, but for learning and bringing about change in human systems as well. However, there is a vast difference between feedback systems for control and feedback systems for change.

Arising from Lewin's professional interest, and in conjunction with others—Leland Bradford, Ronald Lippitt, and Kenneth Benne—field studies for reducing tensions between persons with different group affiliations were attempted. Among those found most useful were direct face-to-face confrontations between people of different religious faiths who, on learning something about the private reac-

---

[3]Norbert Wiener, *Cybernetics: Or Control and Communication in the Animal and the Machine* (New York: Wiley, 1948).

[4]W. Ross Ashby, *Design for a Brain* (New York: Wiley, 1960).

[5]Kenneth D. Benne et al., *The Laboratory Method of Changing and Learning* (Palo Alto, Calif.: Science and Behavior Books, Inc., 1975), pp. 4–5.

tions of others toward them, came to a better appreciation of what they shared in common as contrasted with the ways in which they were unique and different. As a result of this early effort, the impact of feedback became evident. Though its value for control is obvious, its value for problem solving through learning to bring about change remains to be fully realized. The potential is great.

There are four broad classes of critique technique: inspection, simulation, participant observation, and strategic assessment.

Inspection

Inspection is relied on when experience is studied by outsiders—people who are neither involved in nor responsible for the situation itself. Outsiders may study any or all five aspects: products, performance, procedures, process, or people. Officials poring over financial records of a government come to mind as an example. The officials' intention is to be assured that the department's accounting conforms with established procedures. The goal is not to detect wrongdoing, though this may be a result. The purpose is to generalize from what they study to verify that standards are being maintained and to reduce the likelihood that difficulties will be encountered in the future. Beyond that, though, better understanding of what can happen in a given situation may result in generalizations which lead to new accounting procedures.

Simulation

A second critique technique involves simulation. There are many circumstances or situations in which a simulation approximates an actual situation, yet it is not the real thing. The critique of a simulation may be carried out by outsiders, by those engaged in the simulation itself, or by those responsible for applying what is learned from it. Astronauts practicing moon walks in Arizona provide a vivid example, and generals appraising war games, another. A utility company responding to a hypothetical hurricane alert or a fire drill in school demonstrates the use of simulation to identify problems and avoid real difficulties in the actual situation by planning to deal with them in advance.

Participant observation

A third method of critique involves those who are engaged in an activity also being briefed to be observers of the problem solving as it takes place. This is participant-observation critique. Participants critique their own experience in an activity and how they reacted to the events that occurred. Having studied the experience, these insiders diagnose its meaning and generalize from it for the purpose of better problem solving and for assisting others who are faced with comparable circumstances. Sometimes only certain insiders are asked to participate while also observing and diagnosing what is going on, rather than simply to take part in the activity itself. This is still participant observation, but of a particular kind.

Strategic assessment

A fourth approach to critique involves strategic assessment. In this approach a number of people share in setting up, in advance, specific critique strategies and then apply them at scheduled checkpoints along the way, or when critical events occur. Observations are made to test how well specific hypotheses, models, theories, or principles account for what is going on; or data are gathered that lead to the formulation of hypotheses, models, theories, or principles. In several respects the strategic assessment concept of critique is similar to the scientific method model of learning. Often, however, the scientific method cannot be used because the introduction of controlled circumstances or experimental variations is not possible. Hypotheses, models, theories, or principles can, however, be employed to establish specified comparisons in terms of discrepancies or disparities between an actual experience and an alternative, or ideal, one. The results of these comparisons provide material for learning from actual happenings and for introducing changes needed to strengthen the situation.

The swine flu inoculation program in the winter of 1976 demonstrates an application of strategic assessment. A medical hypothesis resulted in a mass inoculation project, with tracking of actual results against those projected for persons of the same age who had been inoculated compared with those who had not been inoculated. Though the program ran into a number of operational difficulties and results are not yet available, an eventual comparison of ideal with actual results will tell how well this approach solved the problem.

Inspection, simulation, participant observation, and strategic assessment, then, are *four* strategies of critique. Each is useful under certain circumstances, but a most important distinction between them is in the notion of single- versus double-loop learning.

What is the difference? Consider, for example, a situation involving two people. One is performing an activity; the second is inspecting the activity in the light of a preestablished set of standards such as accounting principles or medical diagnostic procedures. This is single-loop learning when the second person draws conclusions and reports them to a third person. The learning acquired by the second person does not help the person who has been performing the activity to change, at least in any direct way. Though the performer may get some incidental learning benefits, the purpose of the feedback is to evaluate independently whether or not the performer is in line, and, if out of line, to bring him or her back into line. The performer may get some learning when called in and given an evaluation, but any learning that may happen in this way is purely incidental. The performer is likely to react to the evaluation as being external rather than a part of his or her own experience.

Double-loop learning occurs when the person performing an activity engages with the person studying it to learn directly, rather than indirectly or secondhand. In the double-loop case there are two learners; in the single-loop case, only one. Under these conditions learning can go far beyond evaluation of performance against preestablished standards or goals, and can broaden its focus to evaluate the entire system in which the performer is embedded. It may even challenge an investigator's assumptions about a situation and, hence, the perspective from which it is being viewed.

This distinction between single-loop and double-loop learning is important; it will be developed in later chapters. Inspection, for example, is single-loop learning, while participant observation is double-loop learning.

Examining Different Situation Attributes

We will now describe in more detail the indicators which lead a person to diagnose a situation as having indeed a problem that needs to be solved. Without regard for the particular structure of work, it may be best approached by studying aspects such as product, performance, procedures, processes, and people.

Product

A product is something that can be thought of as having an established existence "out there," independent of those who created it or are responsible for its existence, continuance, or maintenance. Sometimes a product is the outcome of a complex industrial operation. "This detergent is not supposed to leave rings, but it does." The focus of attention is then directed to the product itself and the consequences resulting from its use. Is it a bad chemical formulation? Are there unusual impurities in the water? By searching for possible explanations and causes, it becomes possible to learn from the experience and to pinpoint corrective actions. "This gasoline has an unusual smell," or "I don't know why this can opener doesn't work. Kitchen products from this company are usually reliable."

Sometimes a product may be an artifact, or a thing. Sometimes its existence is simply a result of the direct action of some specific individual, group, or social unit without mechanical supports or the use of equipment. "What a book! It's so good the author must have devoted her life to writing it," or "Lincoln's Gettysburg Address is inspiring. Why did he write it that way?" When a product is of this kind, we cannot examine the actions of its creator during the problem-solving process. Therefore the product itself—the book, the speech—has to be the subject for analysis. "Charlie wrote this letter to me last week. I don't understand what he meant. How do you interpret it?"

Performance

Performance can be observed whenever some result arising from an activity can be identified. "He ran the 100-meter dash in 10.3." "The company produced a return on investment in 1975 of 7.6 percent." "She got a B in biology." Each of these indicates a performance that may reveal the presence of a problem. It is not necessarily a direct observation of the problem itself. None of them tell, for example, how the performance was achieved. But they and many other such indicators are useful starting points for critique when the performance attained is different from that which is desired.

Procedure

All problem-solving activity is organized to provide a basis for regularity. The regulations we use are often referred to as procedures. Some procedures are informal, some formal. *Robert's Rules of Order* in the United States and the parliamentary procedures of Great Britain are sets of such procedures. The countdown for a moon shot is another. Procedures often emerge in an evolutionary way, reaching their final form by trial and error. Often they are accepted unquestioningly because no one has really thought about them or their impact. The way a bed is made or how the dishes are washed are examples of such automatic acceptance.

Paying little or no regard for the time being to performance, or to the specific products which result from performance, problem-solving attention can profitably be focused exclusively on learning from procedures themselves. A business executive says, "Our committee meetings are conducted from an agenda, but there is never enough time to discuss all the items. Too many issues that should be acted on are left undiscussed. We have agreed to abide by them, but are our procedures too mechanical?" A student says this about a problem situation, "I study three hours a night, but I still don't seem to learn much. I catch my mind wandering, but still . . . I love to have the TV on." Another says, "I read my assignments; the first one I study is that assigned in my first class, the second in my second class, and so on. I don't underline, take any notes, or make outlines, but I try to remember what is written as I read it. I rehearse what the book says by explaining it to myself." Such mechanical procedures may account for this student's not learning much from homework. Critique applied to such study practices might make the critical difference—TV or radio on, mechanical reactions to assignments, no underlining, no notes, no outlines, and so on.

When statements about a problem are questioned in an objective way, even by self-evaluation, critique is being applied to the procedures under which the activity is being regulated. The assumption is that procedures themselves may be causing problem-solving difficulties. Once causes have been identified, the procedures themselves can be changed and improved. Then better performance may be expected. For example, a standard operating procedure may be that any purchase larger than $1,000 must be authorized at the next higher level. With inflation, that limit can require department heads to spend time approving relatively trivial purchases rather than doing important work. The solution is to change the procedure by increasing the amount that can be spent autonomously. Critique is a useful way to concentrate on procedures and practices since it increases the possibility of learning from the effects of the procedures themselves how to improve them.

Process

Process is another aspect of experience. Process is concerned with how those responsible for a performance, product, or procedure interact with one another as they engage in problem-solving activities. Sometimes such a process takes place among individuals who need to exchange information and to understand each other. "Bill goes up to see the boss about my increase, but the boss does not even listen. He gets turned down flat with no reason why." The speaker's remarks describe a process of interaction between Bill and his boss. It suggests that the no-increase decision is unrelated to the merits of the case but was caused by an unsatisfactory interaction or social process between Bill and his boss. Critique to learn about a process problem can be useful for improving the quality and outcome of future interactions. Following this improvement, the question of the increase can be resolved on the basis of its real merits.

Here is another example of social process. "Whenever a new topic is introduced, the executives start yelling at one another, and the meeting ends up in chaos." Whatever the reasons may be, the introduction of a new topic may challenge traditional ways of discussion or stimulate competitiveness and noncooperation among members. The implication is that shouting at one another reveals mutual suspiciousness, win/lose attitudes, and so on. This social process reflects problems that can be studied for critique learning of the causes underlying it. The likelihood is that success in solving the problems the critique highlights will result in improved decision making and better results.

People

A fifth attribute of experience that can be concentrated on for critique purposes is people. "Jane has been quiet lately. It's not like her. What's wrong with her?" Now the focus is an observed change in Jane's behavior and performance between one time and another. The change suggests Jane's functioning may be below her norm and possibly related to some personal difficulty that has caused her to withdraw into herself, rather than being free and open in her usual way. If the assumption is correct, Jane (through critique offered by others or by self-examination) can learn more about her problem and the impact her behavior is having on others. She will then have a basis for changing her behavior to what it should be, if she is to make a more effective personal contribution.

Summary

Classifying these five aspects—performance, products, procedures, process, and people—permits major facets of a total experience to be subjected to critique. However, emphasis on any one aspect may result in an entire experience being defined in terms of that aspect only. It gives only a limited view of a situation, and there is risk of losing perspective of the whole by concentrating on one particular part. There may be no real choice, however, other than examining first one aspect, then another, and so on, and in this way identifying the key elements that account for and are basic to an understanding of the whole. Thereafter, a systematic examination and critique of the five kinds of experience together make it possible to differentiate, in each given case, between those that are important and those that are less so. It can also facilitate the examination of one problem at a time, and then provide a comprehensive understanding of a whole set of experiences.

Not all aspects of a problem analysis are of equal importance when compared with others. Judgment is often necessary to concentrate critique on whatever is most likely to promote learning and change. There is no certain way to say in advance that one aspect is more likely than another to yield solutions. Three of the five aspects —products, performance, and procedures—are in a certain sense external. They are the end results of behavior, rather than behavior itself. Because they are often quantifiable in an objective sense and consequently seem to be easier to tackle, critique is sometimes concentrated on them to the exclusion of other aspects of the situation that might, in fact, be much more significant for containing the key to understanding, learning, and improvement.

The other two aspects—process and people—are internal to behavior itself. In a certain sense, process and people are always responsible for product, performance, or procedural difficulties. Thus process and people may be the most significant factors affecting performance in a given situation and, many times, are likely to be the most productive sources of critique learning. For example, problems with a product that critique may help to solve may arise from previously known factors such as temperature, humidity, power interruptions, and so on. However, even in these cases the adverse impact on a product may have resulted from problems existing with the process and people aspects. For example, procedures for controlling adverse influences may have been unused or unavailable. Subordinates may have known what was going on, but because of poor interaction between themselves as well as with the boss, they may have "let it happen." The operator in the situation may have been aware of the problem but may also have been so burdened with personal difficulties as to be unable to really concentrate on the task at hand. Thus, concentrating exclusively on the performance, product, or procedural aspects of a situation could obscure the more likely sources for learning how processes between people, or the personal difficulties of the people involved, are influencing outcomes.

We are likely to avoid the more personal side when social processes and the characteristics of individual behavior are the focus of critique. It is easy, for example, to evaluate a procedure in a neutral, objective way, but it is much more difficult to take the same stance in evaluating human behavior. The threat to mutual understanding and acceptance among participants themselves becomes more intense when processes of interaction and the attitudes and behavior of individual people are studied as the focus of critique.

This is why critique of social process and of persons, unless it is carried out in a climate of trust, confidence, and mutual support, can quickly turn into win/lose power struggles. These, in turn, can make all future social processes within a group even less effective.

Under such circumstances the conclusion may be drawn that it is better to leave the more personal side alone and to apply critique only to those aspects of experience that can be dealt with in more rational and objective terms. If this is done, the answers reached may be false. If critique is applied to processes and people also, the real problems that account for the conditions existing can be examined and changed.

Management Functions

Any human situation that lies somewhere along the structure of work continuum, from completely discrete and unique to completely fixed and repetitive, is managed to some degree. It has in it the elements of order, character, sequence, program, or design, present because of deliberate or spontaneous efforts to avoid confusion or disorder. These elements are essential to prevent the loss of control that arises from a lack of foresight and flexibility. Developing and maintaining order, character, sequence, program, or design involves managing. In this sense persons may manage their day, aircraft commanders a plane, students their homework, supervisors a detergent manufacturing operation, and salespersons their territory. Five interrelated aspects are involved in managing any human activity: planning, organizing, staffing, directing, and controlling.

Planning
Planning takes place whenever effort is directed toward establishing what is to be done before doing it. Setting a goal is part of planning, as is deciding on the steps to be taken to reach it.

Organizing
Whenever someone thinks about how to put together the various activities that need to be undertaken and the patterns of cooperation to be employed in carrying them out, an organizing process is

under way. The coordination of specialized experts and how each person's contribution is dovetailed with that of others is an aspect of organizing.

Staffing

A third attribute of managing situations is staffing. This means answering the question "Who is to be involved?"

Directing

Directing occurs whenever one instructs oneself or others in what is to be done when, how, and why.

Controlling

Controlling means ensuring that plans are being implemented in intended ways, that is, that those who are intended to take part are involved and interacting with one another in completing the task in designated ways, and are either producing expected results or making the changes found to be required.

Planning, organizing, staffing, directing, and controlling are essential components in managing any work structure. Difficulties recognized in performance, products, procedure, process, or people may arise from faulty planning, poor organizing, inadequate staffing, inadequate supervision, or failure to check whether results are in line with what was intended.

Problem solving through critique by evaluating performance, product, and so on in order to diagnose in clear terms what the difficulty is, provides a basis for finding solutions in a better way. Is the *real cause* of the problem one of planning, organizing, staffing, directing, or controlling? After an answer to this question is found, it is possible to introduce needed changes.

Summary

Learning better problem solving from experience is one of the most underutilized and yet most powerful ways for strengthening individual and organizational effectiveness.

Three different work structures—discrete projects, cyclical activities, and continuous flow situations—have been described.

How one particular strategy of critique may be a better approach to learning from one structure as compared with another was discussed. Specific alignments between work structure and critique approach were suggested and evaluated.

The dimensions of critique—*what* is investigated, what *aspect* of managing situations is pinpointed, and *how* it is evaluated—interact with one another to produce learning. The rate at which individuals change through learning can then be plotted.

In the same way, learning curves can be plotted for organizations. The faster the rate of learning, the more successful the organization is. The reason is obvious. When increased understanding exists, fewer mistakes are made, more opportunities are seen, better decisions are taken, and problems get solved.

TWO

Inspection

As a strategy of critique learning, inspection is most likely to be applied to products, performance, or people in order to increase their effectiveness in any one of the management functions of planning, organizing, directing, staffing, or controlling. Inspection in this context means critical viewing or investigation, especially an official examination. Modern legislation appears to be relying more and more extensively on the use of inspection for measuring legal compliance.

A key issue of this approach to critique is *who* learns from inspection. More often than not, learning is acquired by whoever authorizes or carries out the investigation rather than by those whose performance, products, procedures, process, or people are evaluated. There are several approaches to inspection as a mode of critique. These include assessment by experts, commissions, boards of inquiry, debriefings, constant surveillance, and monitoring. All have in common the single-loop concept of feedback.

Expert inspection

Performance, products, and procedure are particularly amenable to problem solving by expert inspection. The reason is that each can be seen or measured in a more or less objective way by persons outside the situation who can view the results from a consistent perspective. Take, for example, end-result performance such as percent return on investment or a commercial airline crash. Performance in cases like these can be studied against preestablished standards or in terms of what might reasonably have been expected under the circumstances which existed at that time. Sometimes inspection is planned, programmed, and scheduled in advance, but not always. Sometimes inspections are formal, for example, planned audits; they may be informal; or they can take the form of unannounced spot checks. Whatever the case, inspection is made by the top person or someone acting on his or her behalf. The inspector usually can command access to whatever evidence or data are pertinent to this study, and the findings are reported to the responsible person. Based on what is learned from the inspection, the authority receiving the report acts on the conclusions reached. If what is learned suggests corrective steps to rectify the identified problems, it is expected that they will be taken to create more favorable conditions.

This expert inspection method of critique is widespread. Inspectors, for example, run checks on continuous activities such as assembly line production, from soft-drink cans to TV sets. When problems are identified and tracked down, a determination is made as to whether the problem lies within the process of management, arises from lack of control or direction, or was brought about by staffing or by some other cause. The corrective action may be better management, or it may be that the producers need to acquire greater skill. In the first case, the role of feedback is emphasized and this may be a supervisory or a "learning how" problem. In the second case, the emphasis is on the need for the producers to learn to perform according to the required standards.

Comments from a self-appointed expert after the event has occurred is a more or less informal inspection. It implies someone adopting an "I judge you" position, suggesting a superior wisdom as to why something did not work out. This form of commentary is usually not intended to provide a genuine critique or learning experience, but rather seeks to find fault with the performance. Therefore it is not likely to lead to change and points to one of the significant differences between critique and evaluation. "Monday morning quarterbacking," often mentioned in the United States, is a good example of this approach.

Commissions

Commissions are appointed under public or corporate authority. The persons selected as members are those thought, first, to be experts regarding the subject to be inquired into and, second, to be above bias. Because the study areas of a commission are usually broad in scope, several persons are appointed. In this way the relevant specialist knowledge thought necessary for carrying out a comprehensive inquiry can be utilized. Commissions are one of the principal ways governments can learn about the functions of their institutions. Commission recommendations often serve as the basis for seeking to rectify weaknesses, and sometimes even for changing basic direction. They may be employed, as was the Warren Commission in the Kennedy assassination, to study and draw final conclusions regarding a significant event. Public commissions usually operate with investigatory powers to obtain and explore feedback from knowledgeable persons as to the facts and data they have which relate to the problem in hand. They report their conclusions and recommendations to the convening authorities, with reasons and evidence to support them. Based on what is learned, the commission may make suggestions for legislation or administrative procedures designed to avoid problems in the future.

Commissions are based on the apparently rational concept of learning that "once reasons are understood, conclusions will be accepted and recommendations for change will be implemented." Though a commission itself usually operates with investigatory powers, a sharp distinction is drawn between the power to investigate and the power to enforce. The power to enforce is usually retained by the body that authorizes the commission.

The Hoover Commission in the United States was established to study government operations and to recommend federal government restructuring in the post-World War II period. An example of the 1970s is the recently completed three-year study of the Australia-Japan relationship, sponsored by the Japanese and Australian governments and undertaken jointly by Sir John Crawford of Australia and Dr. Saburo Okita of Japan.

Many of the recommendations in the Hoover Commission's report were not acted on. Reactions in Japan and Australia to the Crawford-Okita report indicate that the same fate may befall it. This points to an important weakness in the commission approach: a commission's conclusions are often tempered to make them more acceptable to those whose vested interests are threatened by its findings. Because of these resistances, conclusions are filed rather than acted on. The gap between what a commission may recommend as sound and the actual action taken by those who may be called on to implement changes is produced by the fact that those who must make the changes have had little or no opportunity to participate in the thinking and reasoning that led the commission to its conclusions.

Boards of inquiry

Boards of inquiry are also used to investigate some events or series of events in an attempt to relate a given consequence to the causes responsible for it. They usually conduct their investigations on an after-the-fact basis. Investigations by boards of inquiry may be broad or they may be limited to specific issues. For instance, a board might inquire as to whether radar is sufficiently reliable as the basis for instrument landings at military air bases, or why a specific air-traffic accident happened at London Airport at 4:16 p.m. on June 27. A board of inquiry may also, for example, look into the operations of a company with a large government contract where performance is unsatisfactory, costs overruns are being encountered, and so on. In the latter example, inspection is more likely to be used as a control device by the board of inquiry. Whether or not learning occurs is related to the way in which those inspected are able to benefit from the conclusions reached by the board of inquiry.

Boards of inquiry organized to establish the causes of airline accidents are common. Since any given accident may be repeated unless the conditions that caused it are recognized and corrected, all possible causes and influences are taken into consideration. Experts in each area of possible cause serve on the board. Thus an aerial accident in New York was investigated by a board where the conditions examined included weather, electronic communications, the plane's adherence to countdown procedures, traffic conditions at the airport, and other pertinent considerations. By pooling evidence from many different sources, it often becomes evident that some are not pertinent to the outcome, whereas others are critical. Many times boards are able to identify the conditions that account for an accident and can therefore recommend the changes essential for avoiding repetitions.

Debriefings

Debriefing strategies became widely known during World War II and through the space program. To reconstruct significant occurrences that took place between blast-off and recovery, technical experts interviewed astronauts in detail. Debriefings are important because those directly engaged in the situation may be so involved in carrying out their primary duties that they have little time for observing what is going on from a cause-and-effect viewpoint. Debriefing interviews also are a valuable way of gathering data: facts, attitudes, opinions, and points of view difficult to report as they occur. It is important that such information become available to derive the fullest possible learning from the entire experience. The conclusions reached represent important factors for reinstructing those engaged in the experience so they perform differently in the future, or they may become documentation for what to do and what not to do in similar situations in the future, regardless of who is to be engaged in them.

This use of debriefing is for studying cause and effect and in supplementing other evidence of what happened through acquiring additional data, including attitudes. Another advantage may be gained by focusing on something that occurred but was ignored because it did not seem important at the time, or something that happened but was misinterpreted. In this way the record can be set straight and future operations improved.

Debriefings have applications in business and commerce. One application is interviewing sales representatives and others who can report on what is occurring outside the organization itself. It is possible in this way to study market trends, reactions to competitor products, reactions to newly launched products, union and management problems, and so on. Though in some other respects similar to the inspection method of critique, debriefing strategies rarely are as successful when conducted "under authority" as they are when carried out in a climate of helpfulness, mutual research, and investigation.

Constant surveillance

The kinds of inspection described above are conducted on a periodic basis or as single activities. Additionally, inspection can take the form of continuous, ongoing surveillance.

The parliamentary role as set down for committee work in *Robert's Rules of Order* in the United States is an example of inspection by constant surveillance. In this respect, the parliamentarian becomes an inspector-judge who can intervene under his or her own authority and on his or her initiative to rule an activity out of order. The basis, however, of the intervention is an inspection limited to determining the extent to which the operations of the committee have conformed to the specifications for decision making set out in *Robert's Rules of Order*. In addition, any member of the committee can at any time ask the intervening parliamentarian for a ruling as to the propriety of some procedure being followed, or contemplated, so as to obtain a ruling as to its relevance. In this instance, the parliamentarian is more often used as a control device. Any learning benefits are of the single-loop variety since there is no provision for the Rules to be changed—only temporarily suspended under fixed conditions.

The Westminster equivalent to the intervening parliamentarian is the Speaker of the House. In terms of critique, under the United States and Westminster systems, the problem-solving aspects are likely to be confined to practice and procedure, to the neglect of product, performance, process, and people.

Monitoring

Strategies of problem solving are frequently implemented by use of a monitor. It is the monitor's task to evaluate from beginning to termination the extent to which implementations meet the requirements of the agreed-on model. The difference between monitoring and constant surveillance is that the monitor is more likely to check on a periodic or random schedule, while constant surveillance is a 100 percent check.

Failure to meet specifications may be discussed by the monitor with those responsible for carrying out the implementation, or alternatively, the monitor may review deviations with those responsible for enforcement.

As such, monitoring is a special case of inspection and differs from other examples of inspection by being at planned intervals rather than a spot-check or a one-shot approach.

How to Conduct an Inspection

The following guidelines indicate how to conduct an inspection. They apply to inspection in general as well as to special applications through use of experts, boards of inquiry, commissions, and so on.

1. Preestablished standards are available which provide orientation for the project and are understood by those being inspected.

2. Those engaged in an inspection have no responsibility for the activity being inspected.

3. An outsider is said to be needed because insiders are thought to lack objectivity or because of suspiciousness that the insiders can't be trusted.

4. The inspector is credible to those to whom the inspection report will be made and to those whose performance is inspected. That is, the inspector is external and observes the situation that is to be inspected.

5. The inspection is conducted as soon as possible after the happening has occurred.

6. The more the inspection involves realities that are significant in the lives of the people concerned, the more likely the results will be of relevance.

An inspection is announced in advance so people can anticipate it. Alternatively, it is carried out so the people who are to be the subject of the inspection do not have prior warning of it. There is no clear-cut statement as to which is preferable. Sometimes an inspection can only be done on an after-an-announcement basis. Furthermore, an inspection which is "sprung" may create secondary effects that are more adverse than the problem the inspection is intended to solve. Each consideration has to be weighed in the context of the circumstance itself.

Ordinarily, inspectors respect protocol whenever possible in exercising what may legally be their prerogative—that of being outside observers. So far as possible, inspectors avoid conducting "inquisitions" to acquire information. They limit their inspections to those variables that are pertinent to the purpose of the investigation. The investigation is thorough, not only in respect of data, but also so that those who are likely to be influenced by the result of the inspection respect the credibility of the findings.

The report of an inspection, if made verbally, is given immediately or as soon as possible after the inspection and verified by written report. Here is one inspector's description of his duties as an illustration of the use of inspection for problem solving which illuminates some of the strengths and limitations of this approach.

> Our company, being multi-national in character, is confronted with all of the problems of sound and ethical financial management that confront any large company operating in many countries.
>
> We have a Vice President of Finance and direct line channels between him and the financial officers of the various companies. Yet it was felt sometime ago that an independent internal auditing group should be established. This was done and I was made its head.
>
> The mission we have from the Board of Directors is to conduct whatever audits are seen as necessary and sufficient for ensuring that sound and ethical financial practices are characteristic of the operations of this company wherever its business is conducted.
>
> In discharging this responsibility, we travel extensively throughout the free world, sometimes on a solo basis and sometimes as small audit teams. Occasionally we announce a coming visit, though it has become a matter of policy with us not to indicate the specific purposes for which our visit is designed. The reason is that if we warn the organization we intend to audit of the nature of our concern, we can never be satisfied that the documents we are provided have not been developed to meet the questions we are expected to ask. We feel that without such warning we are better able to conduct an independent and authentic inquiry.
>
> At other times we arrive at a subsidiary location unannounced and sometimes we proceed to conduct the inquiry for which we have come immediately after making our presence in the organization known to the chief operating officer. Occasionally we do so by direct contact with the people in the accounting operations from whom we must gain access to data. We report our conclusions to the Vice President of

Finance in the Headquarters operation in New York and to no one else. This is necessary to ensure that what we do is truly an independent audit. It is done in this way so that our staff group does not become a supervisory organization for correcting line deficiencies. Yet it is unfortunate that we must proceed in this manner in the sense that many times it leaves the people we have inspected on tenterhooks.

You asked how we are reacted to in the many operations of our company that we have audited in this manner. I would say we are not an admired group. Rather the opposite is true. Substantial fear surrounds our activities. It may be inevitable that an inspection function such as ours results in a polarization and with us being seen as enemies by the various financial groups. However, I am not satisfied that this is inevitably so. It might be, at least on a hypothetical plane, that the financial operations of various organizations around the world would see us as helping them to maintain sound and ethical operations rather than seeing us as enemies who come in to "catch them."

We are experimenting in three locations to evaluate the possibility of being able to shift from a feared organization to one that is seen as helpful.

Strengths and Limitations

Inspection, then, is a tool for determining whether product, performance, or other attributes are deficient against preestablished standards. It supports the concept of management by exception. It is also a tool for correcting a situation, as necessary, through use of the control function of management. This latter use needs to be contrasted with other forms of critique in which participants study their own behavior and results against preestablished standards and learn in such a way that external or imposed control does not have to be used to change the situation.

Inspection is useful when a tragedy has occurred and no other means of reconstructing the possible causes is available. It is also valuable when expertise is indispensable to a valid evaluation but is unavailable among those who are being inspected. This means that the inspector is qualified in two ways: knowledgeable about the performance, product, or procedure being inspected, and skillful in such analytical techniques of inspection as interrogation, how to recognize and resolve contradictions, and how to write a report.

Inspection is useful when prompt and timely learning is needed and can be a quick fact-finding mechanism.

An advantage of inspection is that inspectors have no vested interests in the conclusions they reach. They can bring expert knowledge to bear on the solution of a problem and thus are able to pursue the inquiry in a more objective way to valid conclusions. A limitation is that they may give more or less importance to subjective and personal factors than they merit. Inspection techniques can probably do a better job in identifying the factors responsible for difficulties in product, performance, or procedure than the internal factors that are accountable for process problems or people variables.

An inspection approach is advantageous when a split has developed between those directly engaged in the experience and those at high levels in the organization who evaluate it. In such a case it may be possible for the independent inspectors to maintain a more neutral stance in evaluating what actually occurred and in helping those involved to learn from the experience. Additionally, a split sometimes makes it possible to use inspectors who are truly expert in comparison with the operators. Using them may be the only way to approach problems that are complex, because the inspectors are not involved in the split and can cooperate, each contributing expertise to achieve a total view. They are therefore able to inquire into aspects of the operators' experience that the operators themselves and the original evaluators are incapable of evaluating.

Conditions favorable to the use of inspection are when:

- Time is unavailable for other methods and fact finding is mandatory.
- Those inside the situation are emotionally involved and therefore their own objectivity cannot be expected.
- Inspectors can provide direct feedback of evidence and conclusions to those inspected.
- Inspectors are accepted by those inspected as neutral, objective, and expert.
- Those inspected are so occupied by executing the situation itself that they have an insufficient opportunity to step back and observe it.

■ It is required by law, which can result in insiders respecting its legitimacy.

Limitations, however, include situations in which the standards may not have been agreed on, or those being inspected do not understand what standards are being applied. In addition, inspectors frequently work with secondhand evidence, particularly when the inspection endeavors to reconstruct experience in order to learn from it. If they have preconceived ideas as to what might have happened rather than knowing what actually happened, these notions are likely to have an adverse influence on the interpretations drawn.

People whose performance is being evaluated rarely learn much from an inspection simply by being interrogated. Others may learn from an evaluation report such as a recommendation or a reprimand. When they do learn something that increases real understanding, it usually is a consequence of the way in which they are asked to make changes as a result of an inspector's recommendations. However, they may still repeat their mistakes. This possibility is reinforced by the fact that inspectors, particularly if they are critiquing a negative situation, are likely to create defensiveness in those responsible for operations. The evaluation is then resisted and rejected rather than being accepted and used as a basis for problem solving in a constructive and cooperative manner. This weakness is characteristic in any situation in which those who study an experience to learn from it are *not* the same individuals as those responsible for conducting the operation itself. The exception to the latter, of course, is when those who inspect are prepared to use or are backed up by enforcement power to ensure that the conclusions reached are brought into operation.

An additional limitation inherent in inspection-based methods is that they are almost always applied after the fact rather than in anticipation of a problem or during a period of ongoing activity. The learning produced can therefore have no effect on current performance or a completed project, and contribution is in terms of rectifying difficulties that might be anticipated on future occasions. Still another limitation is that those whose experience is critiqued do not learn critique methods of learning for themselves. They may remain as incapable of using critique methodology as they were before the inspection was undertaken.

Conditions are unfavorable to the effective use of inspection when:

■ Inspectors themselves may have built-in biases.

■ The inspection process causes a halt in operations and therefore a slowdown occurs when it takes place.

■ It implies that the integrity of the people involved is at issue.

■ Those to be inspected are distrustful and suspicious of the rationale behind the inspection and therefore withhold open collaboration.

■ It is important for participants to learn how to learn rather than simply being told what they are doing incorrectly.

■ Alternative methods are available which produce better results than those resulting from inspection.

■ The circumstances are of such a routine character that inspection can contribute little from a learning point of view.

■ The contribution inspection can make is primarily oriented to external control.

Summary

Some aspects of inspection can be summarized through a brief overview of this approach to critique.

The inspector (commission, board of inquiry, debriefing expert, and so on) acts to evaluate whether some end result in terms of product, performance, or procedure is being reached according to preestablished standards. The inspector gathers data (asks questions, examines records, etc.) to gain insight into the structured activities, whether discrete, applied, or continuous. The questions are answered fully or partially. These answers constitute feedback. Expectations—based on purpose, goal, or question—then are confirmed or not confirmed in some degree.

Learning occurs when satisfactory explanations have been reached for why the expectations that existed were or were not confirmed. Then it becomes possible to draw the following conclusions:

■ *Correlation:* "There are five indications of low morale in the supply department."

■ *Cause and Effect:* "The actions taken are congruent with the mission; all is in order."

■ *Hypothesis:* "The commanding officer has turned sour on military service as a career."

■ *Principle:* "Lowered morale is an inevitable result when leaders lose commitment."

■ *Management implications:* "The commander's leadership has created serious problems of organizing, directing, and controlling. He appears unaware of the severity of the problem. Therefore, we recommend he be replaced."

Inspection appears to be more suitable for gaining insight into performance, products, and procedures, and less suitable for investigating problems that arise from social processes or people. Nonetheless, inspection methods of learning may be useful for deriving conclusions about all aspects of managing situations: planning, organizing, staffing, directing, or controlling.

The major limitation inherent in inspection-based critique is that it usually relies on single-loop learning as the basis for bringing about change. This means that those involved in the situation being inspected have little or no opportunity to influence what the expert inquires into or concludes as a result of the inquiry. A secondary learning benefit to those involved in the situation does come about, but only as a result of new instructions about how to do things differently.

Inspection is most feasible under certain conditions. One is when the problem to be learned about has already occurred and the inspection method is employed for the purpose of reconstructing cause and effect relationships that may account for the problem. Inspection methods also are useful when no one involved in the situation can be assumed to have the necessary competence or objectivity to solve the problem by direct application of double-loop critique methods.

THREE

Simulation

Simulation calls for the active participation of the producers themselves in solving the problems they create. The word *simulation* originally meant "something that deceives, is an illusion, or is meant to deceive, as a fraud or imposture." Simulation today is a recognized and respected term, meaning "the investigation of how the real thing will work when it becomes an actuality." Thus, problem-solving methods which utilize simulations test a provisional activity against preestablished standards on a before-the-fact basis of the actual occurrence. If difficulties are encountered in a simulation, the causes of these difficulties can be identified and eliminated before they appear in a more disruptive, often costly, way in the real setting.

Simulation, then, is creating a replica of what is expected to occur. Pertinent variables from anticipated actions, including management functions, are built into the simulation. Therefore, planning, organizing, staffing, directing, and controlling are present in the simulation in the same way they are expected to be in the actual implementation. The objective is to create an operation that identifies the performance, product, procedure, process, and people elements as they will eventually be found in the true operational situation. Then, through critique during and after the simulation, it becomes possible to reexamine all the aspects of planning, organizing, staffing, and so on, and to introduce corrections in anticipation of actual operations. In this way, *learning is in advance of, rather than as a consequence of, the real experience.*

There are three broad classes of simulations: dry runs and dress rehearsals, prototypes and pilot projects, and model building.

Dry runs and dress rehearsals

After plans have made, for what should occur in an operational situation, it is possible to implement them on a dry-run basis or to conduct a dress rehearsal to evaluate and debug any untoward situation before it happens.

Practicing in advance of a football game provides an example of this kind of simulation. One team is assigned to replicate the opposition's expected game plan. The other is coached to overcome the anticipated opposition. Then a game itself is used to dry-run offensive and defensive strategies. When the opposition is well programmed, a close approximation to actual circumstances in the real game is likely to be encountered. Then corrections can be introduced into the game strategy. Performances of specific players can be evaluated in the light of the simulation performance. Dress rehearsals before a wedding ceremony, a formal rehearsal before an actual stage presentation of a play, answering sample test questions before a college examination, mock trials in law school, or pretesting a speech are examples of this process. It does not require a big step in imagination to adapt these analogies, for example, to the activities of a competitor.

Still another example is role playing. A prospective salesperson, for example, enacts a typical sales situation with another person playing the customer. Their performance is subject to critique, either during the portrayal or afterward. In this way the role player can learn from what occurred how he or she was "coming through," as well as ways to alter the sales interview to get better results. This cited use of role playing is typical of its many possible applications for learning purposes. Almost any social situation can be designed to provide a basis for obtaining feedback and critique. The closer the social situation approximates the real one, the more there is a blending of simulation plus process observation that can be described as a combination of critique methodologies (see Chapter 4).

A related example is psychodrama. The difference between it and role playing is that in psychodrama the actor enacts a real-life problem, not with the person who is involved, but with a stand-in; for example, disturbed relations of a teenager with her mother, of a husband with his wife, or of a colleague with an associate. The actor simulates a real situation to analyze the problem and develop alternative solutions to it. Participants are often unclear about the problem that troubles them. Frequently it is cyclical in nature. Psychodrama provides a means of identifying the problem and seeing ways of breaking the cycle. The director of a psychodrama, and often an audience, provide the feedback essential for breaking through whatever is blocking perception and aiding the troubled person to see constructive ways of dealing with the problem.

Prototypes and pilot projects

There are some discrete activities for which there is little or no prior history. Simulation is one of the problem-solving techniques for moving such an activity from hypothesis to operations. By passing through a prototype or pilot project stage, such as building and operating a pilot plant before constructing one which would be hundreds of times more expensive, the feasibility of the entire project usually replicates the anticipated real situation as closely as possible. Testing the pilot makes it possible to identify sound features. Problems and weaknesses contained in the operation of the pilot that otherwise had not been foreseen will also become evident. Corrections can then be introduced before the real operation starts. A prototype is usually an even more tentative version. It may represent only the key outlines of the project or may be constructed on such a small scale that it is a miniature. However, it contains all the major variables positioned to operate as they would in the real case.

Model building

A third simulation strategy involves identifying the known variables in an actual situation and then setting up a hypothetical model within which those variables are expected to operate. Sometimes the soundness of a model can be evaluated after the fact by feeding historical data into it and then determining how well the model predicts what is actually known to have happened. When the model is demonstrated to be accurate and few if any unknown variables are present, the model permits the future to be projected. Consequences can then be anticipated before they occur by examining the model's operation over many years ahead—five, ten, twenty, or more. It thus becomes possible to anticipate what the future is likely to be and to prepare for it in advance. This method of problem solving can be an important basis for learning from hypothetical experience.

Model building of the sort being described is probably best known in economics. One use of it is the Wharton Model[1] for forecasting what the future economy is likely to be, but there are a number of other private, public, and government economic models. Model building is also used in technical fields such as anticipating where to drill for oil or where to prospect for iron ore or bauxite.

A recent expansion in the use of critique on a national scale is the environmental impact study. When limits and standards for some performance have already been established such as through legislation, by exercise of authority, or premised on a widespread consensus any anticipated activity can be evaluated as to whether its consequences would meet or exceed the limits and standards previously set.

Environmental impact studies seek to anticipate consequences of taking an action such as developing a new suburb, creating an industrial zone, or building a lake, before final approval of the activity is authorized. Usually they rely on statistical projections from known parameters, though simulations and hypothetical models may be used to approximate the real-world impact. This approach of learning by anticipation is undoubtedly important and will continue to expand in use.

Forrester's[2] Urban Dynamics is a model for analyzing and describing what causes cities to rise and fall. Rather than replicating

[1]Professor Lawrence Klein, of the Wharton School of Business, University of Pennsylvania, is credited with developing the Wharton Model.

[2]J. W. Forrester, *World Dynamics* (Cambridge, Mass.: Wright-Allen Press, Inc., 1973).

a whole city as a basis for projecting its future, the Forrester model creates a city from empirical data to learn what its basic functionings are. Where this derived model can be demonstrated to be valid, it can become a basis for predicting the future. In a similar way many individual reports of flu—plotted by geography, time of occurrence, intensity, and rates of change—can be used to predict the intensity of an epidemic, its likely spread, and so on, and to dispatch medicine and health officers to where they will be most needed.

One of the better-known applications of simulation is in the use of feasibility studies for evaluating an action prior to making a commitment to engage in it. Feasibility studies are a second-best kind of simulation, however. Often, many of the variables that operate in the real situation and their probable interaction cannot be anticipated. They frequently have to be ignored or treated as constants. As a result, feasibility studies tend to concentrate excessively on financial variables and to leave out marketing and human variables or to treat them superficially. This explains why the findings of feasibility studies are often very different from the real operations which follow them.

The technique also has pertinence for learning how to create and evaluate alternative human experiences. For example, Argyris[3] has produced two models of human relationships. Model 1 is a win-lose competitive model; Model 2 presumes basic cooperation in relationships. In Model 2 participants are open to receive data. Their choices of action are freely made and commitment to action arises within a person rather than being imposed from without. By programming participants to interact in problem-solving situations according to the specifications of these two models and then conducting enactment situations, it becomes possible to verify in a simulation the consequences in terms of human practices of implementing Model 1 versus Model 2. Critique of these consequences makes it possible to learn the advantages and limitations inherent in relying on one model versus the other as the basis for designing future human interactions.

[3]Chris Argyris and Donald Schön, *Theory in Practice: Increasing Professional Effectiveness* (San Francisco: Jossey-Bass, 1974).

A dramatic use of simulation is in a recent demonstration of how a prison culture develops. College students, who had been tested out as average, volunteered to participate. At a somewhat later time, when they were mentally unprepared for it, the police arrested them in their homes, told them of their citizen rights, put them through more or less standard frisking procedures, and took them to "prison," actually a basement of a university building. Their reactions to prison life were to be studied over a period of two weeks, but to avoid real harm, the simulation had to be concluded at the end of one week.

Guards, who also were volunteers, were unaware that their behavior was under scrutiny. Even though both guards and prisoners understood they were participating in a simulation, both quickly came to replicate the culture of prison life—the guards exercised total power and prisoners responded as though totally powerless.

This demonstration via simulation that average people quickly come to act as guards and criminals in real prisons verifies that the behavior and reactions of prisoners to prison life is not because they are communists, blacks, or radicals, but because of the system and the powerful/powerless relationship that it produces.

Many dynamics known from San Quentin to Attica were replicated in this simulation under conditions where cause and effect could be studied. The result is that the simulation is seen as having important implications for prison reform.

How to Conduct a Simulation

The following are steps for designing a simulation. No one step is indispensable. Together they constitute important guidelines for designing a soundly based simulation.

The design of the simulation should reproduce as closely as possible the circumstances that will exist in the real case. The real case, as designed to operate, is broken down into each discernible element. Each element is treated as a module, but eventually placed together in the sequence they will follow in the real case. No significant module is eliminated. Nothing that would be absent in the real case is introduced into the simulation. The temptation to include an additional but false step that will not occur in the real thing, "to take advantage of the extra learning," should be avoided.

Those who operate the simulation are those who will be the responsible operators in the real situation. Each person should have the analogous position in the power-authority system as that for which he or she will be responsible for in the real case. Planning, organizing, directing, staffing, and all other functions are replicated in the simulation as closely as possible to what the real case would be.

Forms, charts, communications, letters, telephone, and other means of interaction essential for operating the simulation are designed to follow what can be anticipated for the real case. Practice sessions as needed to acquaint participants with how the simulation is expected to work should be completed prior to starting the formal evaluation. Criteria for evaluating the learning from a simulation are identified in advance of the simulation's design. They may include: (1) performance, product, procedure, process, and people effectiveness criteria; (2) significant deviations in the simulation from the way it was planned to operate in respect of performance, product, procedure, and people variables; planning, organizing, directing, and staffing deviations; and (3) unexpected sources of variation that were not built into the simulation model.

Strengths and Limitations

An advantage of simulation is that something which does not yet exist, but which is anticipated, can be set up in approximately the form which it is expected to take. Critique can be applied to models in much the same way it can to real circumstances, and often more meaningfully. Thus, it is possible to learn much from replication and thereafter to apply insights to increase the likelihood that real operations will turn out as the model predicts. Of course, the prediction is only as good as the similarity between the variables in the model and those to be found in the actual circumstance.

Simulation is useful when:

■ The variables of a real case are sufficiently predictable so they can be built into a simulation.

■ The end results can be duplicated.

■ Sufficient time exists to change the design of the real case based on results from the simulation.

■ Resources are available to conduct the simulation.

■ The real case has high enough risk factors in terms of performance, product, people, or other variables to justify simulation.

The main disadvantage is that simulations, no matter how realistic they may be or how closely they may approximate the actual circumstances, are not the real thing. This is particularly true when people and their performance, procedures, or processes are involved. For people, simulations often do not have the same significance as real-life operations. They can therefore give false readings.

Simulation is not useful when:

■ A simpler method of learning might yield essentially the same conclusions, such as operating the real case as a trial subject to modification and using participant observation or inspection methods before establishing the final design of the operation.

■ The real case has been so thoroughly worked out either as a modification of some well-founded past experience or in terms of well-known engineering or commercial principles that little learning can be anticipated from the simulation.

■ The real case is so far away from implementation in terms of time that it is likely to be altered based on knowledge yet to come, rather than on findings from a worthwhile simulation.

■ So little is known about the variables that would operate in the real case that simulating them cannot be expected to yield worthwhile results.

Summary

Simulation is a way of studying situations projected to occur in the future by creating the situation under hypothetical conditions, studying how it works, and testing modifications that might make it better.

The key variables expected to be present in the real situation are determined to create a replica, model, or hypothetical version of what might happen in actuality to test the consequences from the simulation. The simulation is first used to plot out what to do. Then expectations based on simulation activity may be used to test how close what is actually occurring is to the anticipated outcome. Expectations regarding how the real situation will operate are confirmed to some degree or they may remain unconfirmed, requiring new effort to learn what is most likely to happen.

Learning occurs when a simulation demonstrates that:

- The anticipated results occurred.

- Unanticipated happenings cannot be accounted for by the variables as built into the situation.

- Variables not recognized in the situation are having significant effects, in which case it may be necessary to redesign the simulation.

Simulation enables those concerned with solving a problem, testing a provisional solution, or comparing alternative possible solutions, to evaluate the relative merits of an already proposed solution. It is an anticipatory method of learning that permits errors to be recognized and eliminated before the real-life situation occurs.

FOUR

Participant Observation

Participant observation is a concept of learning from experience that originated in anthropology. The idea was that real insight into another culture was best acquired by living in that culture and taking an active part in its everyday activities. The task of the anthropologist, then, is to critique the actual living experience and derive from it an accurate description of the particular culture.

As a problem-solving method, it is used by people to study what is happening to themselves and to others while engaged in an activity to increase their effectiveness. In other words, a person becomes a measuring device during an experience through actively observing actions and reactions as they occur.

Participants in an experience usually have little difficulty in describing it, at least in mechanical terms. "We started at ten o'clock and though the project was to be completed by noon, we did not complete it until twelve-thirty." The following is an example of the differences between reporting an event as it occurred and a participant's observation of what went on and why. "Even though I needed to exchange information with Bill and Tom, they never spoke to me or to each other. Bill always had to ask Ned to get the information from Tom, and Tom got his information from Bill through Ralph. By the time it got to me, it was useless." Observing

47

what went on at the process-and-people level, in other words, involves being aware of how and why things are occurring as they are. Reporting is simply reconstructing on a mechanical basis what happened, or observing others solely from a performance, product, or procedure point of view.

As an approach to problem solving, participant observation begins when individuals evaluate their own reactions to an event they have directly experienced or are currently experiencing. Several contributions to learning from it are possible whenever an individual thinks about an experience and makes personal reactions and evaluations known to others in an attitude of openness and mutual respect. An important contribution is identifying and discussing hidden doubts and reservations. When this has been done, insights into why these doubts and reservations exist can be focused on under circumstances where they can be evaluated. If these doubts and reservations are found to be realistic, it then becomes possible to alter circumstances so these doubts are taken into consideration. If they are based on fears and anxieties rather than objective thinking, it becomes possible to help those who suffer doubts and reservations to think through and face up to their feelings so they may become free of negative or restrictive impacts.

The following example is of a work group meeting with a consultant, Jack, who is helping the participants to clarify their feelings and relationships so they can work together more effectively: After a slow beginning, something happened. Jim . . . voiced concern about his relationship with Rod. . . . "What's happened to us? Lately we can't seem to get anywhere on design problems." "Strange," Rod replied. "I've noticed it, too."

Rod explained further that Jim's whole philosophy of management seemed to have changed once Jim was no longer subordinate to him, and this came through to Rod as "dishonest." Jim and Rod tried to clarify this misunderstanding. Other participants stepped in from time to time to assist in this process.

The consultant had been successful in getting these two members of the group involved in critique and feedback, as this dialog illustrates: "If you had only let me know how you felt," Jim implored, "we could have straightened this out long ago." "Well, I got the message that you didn't much care what I thought," Rod countered. "When you invited the engineering people to come to your house for the barbecue, you didn't invite me. I assumed you wanted the opportunity to solidify your position with your new people."

Jim explained that no slight was involved; Rod had not been invited because Jim had understood he would be out of town. As a result of this mutual feedback, the following tension-relieving scene occurred: "The first session ended, and during the coffee break Rod and Jim stood in the hall, drinking coffee and talking busily. Excited, Rod said, 'I'm sure glad we could clear the air! I feel a lot better now that I got it out in the open. I think I can sit down and work with you now. My feelings won't be standing between us.' Rod extended his hand."[1]

This kind of communication about "feelings as data" gives each person the additional information essential for interpersonal problem solving. In this instance, feelings associated with changes in status were in the forefront. By sharing the emotions that each had, and their respective interpretations of events, perceptual clarification was achieved.

Another example occurs when two people observe the actions of a third person and each interprets the meaning and intent of these actions in a different way. By describing and discussing these differences, potential misunderstandings, errors, or other unanticipated consequences can be avoided. In addition, it is possible that neither of the two who differ agree with the third. It is difficult to sort out the resulting confusion unless differences are confronted as they occur, and double-loop feedback is used to clarify action as it takes place.

In the Western world it is often said that the use of committees is very wasteful, as they are rarely effective and their capacity for analyzing problems and reaching conclusions or recommendations sometimes deteriorates to a very bad degree. While the above appears to be a true statement, whether the use of committees is in universities, government agencies, companies, and numerous social and volunteer organizations, the reason for their ineffectiveness

---

[1]A. H. Kuriloff and S. Atkins, "T-Group for a Work Team," *Journal of Applied Behavioral Science*, 2(1): 63–93, 1966.

remains to be explained. Deficiencies in committee functioning are not related to the committee concept itself, but to the failure of committees to rely on any use of critique for identifying the negative trends that are defeating the effectiveness of the committee. Without the capacity for identifying such weaknesses or deficiencies, committee operation rarely improves and often goes from bad to worse.

A committee should be capable of pooling the resources of its members, confronting and relieving disagreements, and in other ways acting in an intelligent manner toward meeting its stated objectives. The fact that it is often unable to do so can only be charged to the deficiencies in the use of critique. As mentioned earlier, parliamentary rules and *Robert's Rules of Order* omit any reference to or utilization of critique for learning and change purposes. Participant-observation strategies are particularly useful for increasing the effectiveness of committee work.

In many countries a similar criticism is lodged against the use of syndicates in college and university settings. A syndicate is a group of students who are expected to collaborate in carrying out an assignment or in preparing an overall paper. Syndicates are rarely successful; often they deteriorate into a series of solo actions, with each person taking an independent piece of responsibility or a particular individual doing more or less the entire project. Here, again, the deficiency seems to be in the failure of syndicate members to utilize critique in order to study the effectiveness of their performance and to rectify weaknesses or deficiencies that arise and become overriding obstacles to syndicate success.

Participant observation can be used at the beginning of an activity, during its course, or at its termination. Critique introduced at the end of an activity permits participants to review and evaluate the entire experience from inception to conclusion. Interpersonal influences can be traced, critical choice points identified and evaluated, recurring patterns verified, and all these related to what actually happened. The insights gained can be significant for cause-and-effect analysis and for deciding what is and what is not the best way to carry out a comparable activity in the future.

Participant observation also has merit when introduced at the beginning of an activity. Participants think about the situation in which they are about to engage and so anticipate what is likely to happen. It is possible in this way to anticipate and thus avoid problems before they become realities. Possible procedures that might be followed can be identified and evaluated. Determining what each participant knows, what each expects to happen, and what each wants to see done, makes better utilization of human resources a distinct possibility.

Participant-observation critique can also occur spontaneously or according to a plan at any time an activity is in progress. These critiques are particularly useful while an activity is unfolding, because unrecognized problems and unresolved difficulties can be identified and corrective actions introduced before adverse effects materialize. This method of critique is especially suitable for evaluating the quality of results and teamwork prior to reaching an end result.

Still another approach is the designation of one member to be responsible for leading the critique, who is not only expected to participate but also to pay particular attention to process and people aspects of group activity. This person leads group discussion at some predesignated time, often close to the end of the meeting, and is expected to focus issues of relevance for discussion. Many participants find this double responsibility difficult to do in a satisfactory way and believe that more progress is made by sharing responsibility with someone in the group, who is also responsible for observing while participating.

The participant-observation approach is best exercised when all team members have some skill in giving and receiving feedback and are prepared to use critique as needed under each of the circumstances described above. Then false starts can be avoided, wrong choices can be eliminated, and a whole activity can be reviewed to determine how to strengthen performance in the next cycle of experience. Participant-observation critique can be impromptu or postmortem, or it can be done through the use of a process observer.

Impromptu feedback

Impromptu feedback is just what the phrase implies: spontaneous, off-the-cuff comments regarding what is occurring. This approach is one where reactions are likely to be people-centered rather than focused on procedures or processes, though these may often be the true sources of difficulties.

Such feedback has value principally by virtue of its spontaneity. More often than not, the remarks made are not well thought out nor are others prepared to accept the validity of the statements. For example, when Tom says to Bill, "You are being dogmatic. You keep on repeating your opinion and haven't listened to a thing I've said," it may be a valid observation by Tom that he isn't being heard but it is not likely to prompt Bill to listen to Tom. Rather, Bill is more inclined to respond to the accusation that he is being dogmatic and deny or justify his behavior. Such interventions are likely to produce defensiveness and injured feelings. Because of its unplanned character, impromptu feedback is unlikely to initiate critique which leads to changes in how situations are being managed from the standpoint of planning, organizing, and other relevant issues.

Here is an example of the impromptu use of participant observation to personal evaluation which occurred during a team meeting and increased the effectiveness of Joe, one of the members.

> *Peggy to Joe:* "Well, getting back to Joe here for a minute. Are you suggesting in effect then that we continue discussion and, as we see people get into a situation, that we stop and test it then and there?"
>
> *Joe to Peggy:* "Well, yes. Take the opportunity to point it out just when it happens."
>
> *Peggy to Joe:* ". . . to observe each other as the discussion goes and see how things turn out. . . . Is that right?" (general agreement)
>
> *George to Joe:* "Let me try one on for size. *I just noticed you jump to an inference, very fast.* . . ."
>
> *Joe to George:* "That's right."
>
> *George to Joe:* ". . . just a second ago . . . and what I meant was— and I can give you an example. *All of a sudden you say, 'Well I've got the answer. It isn't that at all. It's this.' You go too fast for the rest of us.*" (George spots a critical example and calls Joe's attention to it right after it happens.)
>
> *Joe to group:* "Well, do you deduce from that that I'm a man of action? (laughter and some confusion) More seriously, I can understand why I look that way to you. I'll try to watch it, but if you see me doing it again, tell me about it.

With these kinds of evaluatory remarks, the likelihood is increased that Joe can examine his own behavior, including the motivations on which it is based, and ask himself some very pointed questions. Joe then recognizes the specific negative items of behavior that worry others and the positive ones that can encourage them to accept his leadership and to contribute to the problem-solving effectiveness of the team.

Postmortem

Translated from the original Latin, the word "postmortem" means "after death." In the legal sense, postmortems provide one of the principal ways of determining the causes of death by examinations after the event. They are often conducted for statistical and actuarial purposes and to draw cause-and-effect conclusions so that preventive actions can be taken to avoid needless death.

Used in everyday situations, however, a postmortem is a far less legalistic critique procedure. Sometimes conducting a postmortem means little more than a casual attempt to figure out what happened, usually after something negative has occurred. Occasionally, however, organizations or individuals establish the practice of critiquing all significant events, including successful ones, after they have happened. A postmortem, normally, is the natural or expected critique that participants engage in either on a one-to-one basis, or as a group upon completion of an activity or some time later. As participants think about an experience, conclusions regarding performance, or certain critical aspects of it, are reached. These relate particularly to procedures, processes, and people, and sometimes a postmortem can piece together interactions between these three variables and the effect they had on performance and product. The naturalness, as it were, of postmortem critique reflects a need to wind up a person's thinking about an activity before relegating it to memory.

The following is a description of postmortem at work in an organization trying to find out why seemingly clear and logical development plans fell short of the expectations they had created.

MARKETING STRATEGY—WHAT HAPPENED?

In recent years senior management people have worked with the President to define the long-range direction for the Company: Where are we going, and how are we going to get there?

One part of this work was the development of a Marketing Strategy, which was designed to answer these questions: (1) *To whom* do we intend to sell our products? We can't be all things to all people, so how will we concentrate our sales efforts? (2) *How* will we do the selling? Will we use agents, brokers, salaried salespeople, or some other way? (3) How will we *organize* to support the sales efforts?

During 1974, a set of principles was developed to answer these questions. Those involved went on to plan specific action steps to implement these principles. The two parts—the principles and the action steps—were published in a Marketing Strategy designed to inform people in the office and the field about Marketing Strategy and what it meant to them.

The communications program assumed that we were ready to proceed with the action steps outlined in the Strategy document. Many people began to work on making them happen. But something happened along the way and the changes didn't occur. People began asking, "What happened?" The lack of action, coupled with other events discussed in earlier articles in this series, left many people feeling that 1975 was a hollow year. Yet the answer to the question, "What happened?" is important to anyone concerned with the future of the company, so we designed a critique document to enable us to get some answers.

Response

Once the document was published, critique came quickly, from the field and the head office. Among the many valid points raised were these:

■ The original design put the car before the horse by emphasizing a sophisticated set of financial service products before we had developed a sales force big enough and good enough to market them. We had to be sure we did the best job possible selling our existing services before we took on other kinds of services.

■ The initial design emphasized direct sales and appeared to downgrade our sales through brokers. Doing that would run counter to our basic financial objective of doubling income in five years, because a great part of that new income would come from brokered business. We do want to strengthen our direct sales, but we need the brokerage market, too.

■ There was an idealistic flavor to the original document, in part because the action steps were not fully thought through. When work began on implementing them, people quickly found valid reasons why some of the ideas couldn't work.

Loyalty versus Logic

Having received this kind of feedback, we faced a crucial choice: either proceed with implementation, or pause to reexamine the strategy and action steps. It was a "loyalty versus logic" dilemma—to be loyal to one's own work, perhaps blindly so, or to reject emotional attachments in favor of facts, data, and logic. We opted for logic.

It took a great deal of time to do this rethinking—too much time, in fact, and here we made another mistake—we didn't communicate with people about the delay, thus leaving them up in the air. If we could do it all over again, those problems would be avoided. Nevertheless, our marketing approach has been reformulated, and it now is ready to move ahead.

Marketing Strategy Revised

The *strategy itself,* as distinct from *the action steps to implement it,* remains much the same. We will concentrate on serving clients whose income is $20,000 or above (in 1975 dollars). We will build a large, highly qualified, full-time sales force. We will grow while maintaining profitability.

Major changes have been made in the action steps, too. Here is a summary of the new plan:

A dual distribution system has been developed to aim at two market segments: the brokerage (wholesale) business, and the "whole man" (retail) business. Some Group Sales Offices will gradually become Branch Brokerage Sales Offices dealing with the wholesale market as well. They will carry on their traditional approach in the products area and, in addition, will be responsible for securing brokerage business. General Agencies will be formed in new areas to provide a separate facility for satisfying clients' needs pertaining to special categories. We will build on the strengths of our current special agencies in their current locations in both career and brokerage.

The Branch Brokerage Offices and Group Offices will provide training, technical expertise and administrative assistance to our present agencies and to the new type of General Agencies in the sale of Group Products.

All these marketing outlets are vital to the objectives of Marketing Strategy. We must develop a distribution system to concentrate on development of brokerage business. The branch offices will build upon our strengths and success in both our principal markets. The planned addition and expansion of General Agencies will help achieve sales and manpower goals not only in the next five years, but also will build a foundation for the development of a full-time sales force beyond 1980.

The Answer

What Happened to Marketing Strategy? It was created—it was developed—it was formulated—it was communicated—it was critiqued—it was agonized over, sweated over, and finally, it was revised, until it is now being implemented to achieve its purposes.

Here is another view of postmortem critique at work. It comes from a chairman of a company operating as a building and civil engineering contractor.

We made a decision at board level to invest in a certain operation a few years ago which led us to a loss of almost a million dollars.

Our decision to proceed had been unanimous—indeed, unusual for us, we were unanimous about it right from the start—and it was only when things began to go wrong that we realized that at no time during our discussion of the project had we said to each other, "What are your reasons for proceeding and on what assumptions do you base your recommendation to go ahead?"

When we did ask this question—too late, of course, to stop the project without the loss—we found that the reasons and assumptions on which our individual recommendations were based contained so many conflicts, contradictions, and errors that *had we discussed them at first we would never have proceeded with the project.*

As a critique method, delayed postmortems have the limitation that they are likely to be unplanned and recollections may be incomplete. The possibility of making real use of the lessons learned is remote, that is, changes needed in planning, organizing, and staffing, though identified, are unlikely to be put into action. This potential failing has to be avoided through careful planning.

So-called sunset laws represent an example of a postmortem strategy which is introduced not after death, but in anticipation of the end. The "Sunset Law," adopted in Colorado, "would terminate in six years the state's regulatory agencies, representing a third of all its executive units, unless they justify their existence. Some 39 agencies regulating businesses ranging from mobile home dealers to utilities are affected. If an agency fails to convince the legislature it should be reestablished, the agency's sun will set."[2]

[2] R. L. Simison, "New 'Sunset Laws' Seek to Curb Growth of Big Government," *The Wall Street Journal,* June 25, 1976.

Such an approach stimulates critique for self-study in a number of ways. "The concept actually is intended more to force legislatures to review their offspring than to wipe out a lot of agencies."[3] Second, the use of strategic assessment types of critique of the actual-ideal, obligated-actual, and theory versus actual (see Chapter 5) is stimulated to ensure that legislative intent is cemented into administrative practice. Third, ongoing critique is utilized to identify program weaknesses to avoid later adverse reactions. Fourth, various inspection and monitoring strategies are used to ensure that actual activities are congruent with legislative authorizations. Finally, the sunset law strategy stimulates postmortem types of self-examination toward the end of the authorized period so those responsible for other activity can be in a position to recommend termination or justify continuation of the activity through another cycle. "The various Sunset laws seek to use a different mechanism to impose the same result: top-to-bottom reassessment on a regular basis."[4]

The obvious risk in such strategies is that the strategy becomes ritualized and the intended terminal evaluation becomes a form only, whose substance has been lost.

Post meeting reactions

Post meeting reactions (PMR) include a wide range of information-gathering procedures used for purposes of learning how participants reacted to what was going on in a just completed meeting. Once information has been collected and summarized, it becomes possible for participants to use the data as a basis for discussing why the situation was as it was. Then they can review with one another what changes should be introduced to increase their effectiveness. PMR are often collected under conditions of anonymity because it is not then necessary for participants to justify their reactions. The information can be evaluated for its own worth rather than from the standpoint of who felt what or who reacted in what particular way. This approach has a strength and a limitation. The strength is that participants are more likely to reveal their true feelings, unless, of course, they are members of a team where

[3]Ibid.
[4]Ibid.

candor and mutual support already exist in some depth. The limitation is that no one person has the responsibility to stand behind the conclusions that were individually reached, and some comments may range from caprice to malice.

The kinds of questions included in a typical PMR form can focus on such issues as attitudes toward participation; feelings of involvement and commitment to the activity; the extent participants perceived the goals they were working toward were clear; whether decisions reached were on the basis of consensus, compromise, or one person rule; the degree of support for the decisions reached. PMR forms usually concentrate on procedures and processes. Evaluating performance or products on the one hand, or pinpointing specific reactions to individual people on the other, are less likely to be examined by this method.

Process observers

A variant of participant-observation strategy is to ask an individual to remain outside the actual activity and as a process observer observe procedure, process, and people, intervening whenever circumstances reach a point of impasse, indecision, unproductive result, or lowered quality to assist members to solve problems. In addition, the process observer may lead a post-meeting evaluation, often starting it by revealing his or her observations as to what was seen happening and then engaging others in testing the accuracy of these observations, correcting them, and adding to them.

An example of process observation in a one-to-one situation is a flying instructor who may work with a student pilot to critique how the pilot talks to the controller in the tower. The process-observer situation enables the instructor to help the student improve conciseness of communication.

One strength of the process-observer strategy is that a person familiar with the situation may be appointed to observe it while actively participating. An individual given this assignment is able to concentrate on the procedure, process, and people in the interests of improving the effectiveness of the situation. One limitation in this approach is that it is artificial for a person with a stake in an issue to be asked to withdraw from an activity in order to observe it.

How to Conduct a Participant-Observation Critique

Voluntary and willing collaboration among those to whom participant-observation critique is pertinent is essential for the effective use of this method. If people have willingly and voluntarily committed themselves to such participatory problem solving, defensiveness that otherwise prevents learning from occurring is reduced and cooperative attitudes toward feedback are increased. On a voluntary basis, this form of critique shifts from a power-authority kind of implied criticism to a morale-commitment basis of mutual support for achieving positive results through effective teamwork.

Ordinarily, a boss or leader of a group introduces and describes participant observation as a method of problem solving. However, there is no reason why some other member may not be designated to describe the method and thus become responsible for this part of the group's learning.

The second step is for the person responsible to identify the pros and cons of the approach, namely, the advantages and the risks involved in implementing this method under the specific and particular conditions prevailing. Members are then invited to indicate what their own feelings are toward the proposal, in particular, to express whatever reservations and doubts they may have. Going beyond this, members are prompted to explore why they have these feelings and to test after review whether or not these sources of concern have been reduced or eliminated. The designated person then aids the other members to test their readiness to engage in participant-observation–based learning. If participants express their readiness, further steps are taken; if they are reluctant or hesitant, the proposal to initiate the following steps is postponed for future consideration or withdrawn.

If the decision is to go ahead, an initial test period is proposed, say, ten to thirty minutes. At a specified time work is interrupted so participant observers can exchange views on what has been going on. In this way, an experience of how this approach to critique is carried out can be assessed in terms of how team members react to it.

A number of steps are involved in the exchange of observations which the designated person initiates:

1. Important ground rules of observation are agreed on, such as those who speak should do so in descriptive terms and those who listen should do so to understand, rather than evaluate, what is being said.

2. Someone is asked to volunteer observations (perhaps by saying, Who wants to start?). Alternatively, the first and second observers can be selected before the interruption occurs. This may be done by alphabetical order, seniority, or any suitable method.

3. Reactions are monitored. Participants are asked to clarify specific points before inviting others to describe their reactions.

4. Efforts to explain away, to justify, or to rationalize what is being reported are discouraged by saying, Wouldn't it be better to try to *understand* rather than to *judge* or *evaluate* at this stage?

5. Other participants are invited to offer their observations until each person has had an opportunity to report. If there are some who wish to withhold their comments, their desire to do so is respected, though several requests for their views are made, stressing the advantages of gaining insight into the reasons for their reservations and doubts.

Observations may be summarized on flip chart paper to identify common themes and unique reactions. After all observations have been given, the boss or team leader invites participants to summarize by identifying common themes and discrepant observations.

Using what has been learned from the completed critique, the next steps involve planning for improvement. This includes asking participants to suggest how effort in the next period of activity might be made more productive and satisfying, testing for the amount of agreement to acting on the recommendations offered, and helping participants reach agreement on concrete steps for implementing the recommendations. The activity then moves into its next segment of work and the next critique period is scheduled.

After completion of the whole activity, participants critique the effectiveness of participant observation as a basis for learning from experience. Readiness to use participant-observation critique on an ongoing basis is tested by deciding whether or not it should be continued in the next activity. This will provide a sound indicator of its likely worth to each particular group as a method of learning.

Strengths and Limitations of
Participant Observation

The various forms of participant observation share the advantage of ensuring that those whose active participation is under examination become their own examiners and evaluators. It is most likely that the conclusions reached will be implemented, because the procedural and process implications that have been discussed are well understood by virtue of the participants' having experienced them directly prior to discussion.

Some guidelines can assist the use of participant observation in circumstances where it has the greatest likelihood of improving problem solving. A clue that participant observation is needed is that discussion bogs down or members feel progress is not being made. Examples are: when discussion goes around and around on the same issue or jumps from issue to issue without a clear direction being visible.

Ordinarily, the leader takes the initiative to start critique. However, a work group may set criteria by which any member who sees the need can initiate a critique. A sense of timeliness is needed, whether the critique is initiated by the boss or another member. Critique can be started by saying, "Let's stop and check on how we are doing," or by the adoption of any other signal chosen by the group. Once a critique is started, all members should be alert to silent participants and seek out their comments. Silence does not necessarily mean agreement. It may hide deeply hidden resentments that need to be brought to the surface if effectiveness is to be increased.

Under certain conditions, particularly when the performance being evaluated is complex, it is best to record critique points in a way that can be seen by all, such as on flip chart paper. Then specific reactions and evaluations can be analyzed for themes, patterns, and trends. Differences in reactions and evaluations should be identified and discussed to establish whether they are based on misunderstandings or other causes and, if possible, to resolve them.

The team leader needs to be aware (as, indeed, do all members) of the importance of double-checking with all members as to whether there are additional hidden reservations and doubts that need to be brought to the surface, identified, and dealt with before unhampered involvement, participation, and commitment to action is possible.

Critiques are undertaken on a regularly scheduled basis in the conduct of some activities. Additional critiques should be conducted whenever discussion is less open, candid, straightforward, sound, and valid than it should be. As confidence increases in the use and value of critique, it is likely that members will rely less on the boss to initiate this activity. Then all members will take responsibility for introducing critique whenever the need for it is seen.

The following criteria should be interpreted flexibly with regard to the circumstances for the possible use of participant observation for increasing the effectiveness of problem solving:

- When work is bogged down and individuals are unclear about the causes of their lack of progress
- When work practices have been relatively formal and there is a readiness to move toward informality and more spontaneous collaboration
- When better time management is needed
- When a new procedure is being introduced
- When a group is embarking on an innovative activity
- When a group's membership is changed, particularly by the introduction of a new boss
- When it may increase the participant's ownership of the problem
- When it is probably the only way to study process and people problems

There are several limitations of participant observation. The first lies in the difficulty many persons experience, when they are deeply involved in an activity, of being objective and making sound observations at the same time. They are called on to observe as they are participating, that is, to talk and to observe simultaneously. In addition, their own reactions to the activity, as well as to the individuals in it, may color what they think and feel. Therefore, different people are likely to observe different aspects of the situation. This is a strength as well as a limitation because when more points of view are brought to bear on an activity, there is greater likelihood that learning can result.

Second, observation and feedback mechanisms create a need for effectiveness and skill in communication. Participants must be able to develop such skills if the impact of participant observation is to be significant.

Finally, if conditions of mutual trust and helpfulness and a collaborative climate of problem solving are absent (see Chapter 1), participants are unlikely to be able to attain the level of candor and openness that can result in objective evaluation and assessment.

The following conditions are unfavorable to the use of participant observation and limit its potential contribution to problem solving:

- When two or more participants are antagonistic to one another and would use the opportunity of feedback for mutual criticism
- When there is a crisis and the time needed for deliberation is unavailable
- When activities are relatively unimportant or of such a routine nature that few benefits can be anticipated by submitting them to examination and study
- When participants are inexperienced in face-to-face feedback methods or unskilled in open communication
- When participation constitutes an interruption that disturbs a chain of thought

Summary

Participant observation as a method of critique to enhance problem solving can be used in connection with any kind of work, at the beginning, during, or at the end of an activity.

Participants can think through the purpose, goal, or objective of an activity and how it can best be accomplished. This can ensure that all are in agreement as to what should happen and that they are in a position to anticipate and correct problems before they happen to ensure the success of their operations.

Concurrent critique periods interrupt an activity so participants can give each other feedback regarding procedures, processes, or people and whether they are contributing to or hindering performance on the completion of a task. Do they, in other words, impart thrust to the work in hand or do they impose drag and slow it down?

When an activity is completed the performance or product is evaluated to determine whether or to what degree accomplishment was present. Those involved determine whether the accomplishment was satisfactory. If so, why? If not, why not?

Process observation enables conclusions to be reached regarding the procedures and processes utilized and in respect of their application in future activities. Recommendations are made for what each participant might do to strengthen his or her contribution. In these ways participant-observation critique is useful in improving the way people work together as they learn from joint experiences.

FIVE

Strategic
Assessment

There are two broad classes of strategic assessment: action research and discrepancy models. Each is designed around specific, definable, behavioral science concepts of the principles underlying human behavior and performance. They are helpful for learning about what is occurring in given situations and, at the same time, for demonstrating to what degree the conduct being studied departs from sound principles of human behavior and performance.

Action Research

Any organized activity starts with a goal that is to be reached by a pathway or series of activity steps.[1] Sometimes the steps bring about progress toward the goal; sometimes they do not. Also, the progress made may be less than would have been achieved had different steps been taken. Planning is a feasible basis for proceeding toward a goal. In like manner, organizing, staffing, directing, and controlling are pertinent aspects of the total activity between establishing and reaching a goal. By stopping action at designated intervals or whenever there are indications of problems, pathway

[1]Kurt Lewin, "Action Research and Minority Problems," *Journal of Social Issues* 2: 34–46, 1946.

activities can be evaluated by those engaged in them. Adjustments to planning, organizing, directing, staffing, and controlling can then be introduced to eliminate difficulties and to prevent the actual occurrence of anticipated problems.

This kind of critique makes it possible for those engaged in pursuing a goal to interrupt their activities at various points to measure the extent to which they are moving toward or away from the goal; whether their rate of progress is as planned or faster or slower; and whether or not quality is sound. The approach being used to reach the goal can also be assessed to see if it is deficient and to what degree. Staffing to accomplish the goal can be examined to determine whether the requisite knowledge, skills, and attitudes are available. The direction (i.e., leadership or supervision) being exercised for coordinating effort can be evaluated and a decision can be reached as to whether it is too tight or too loose. Finally, the question can be asked, Are these controls providing a sound basis of relating activities with the goal? A typical sequence involved in an action research use of critique is shown in Figure 1.

Goals

On the left side of Figure 1 is the word goal. The goal may be a broad, vague idea, or a specific, highly detailed project to be accomplished. Given changes in the situation, difficulties in predicting the future, or the fact that many situations contain unknowns that cannot be anticipated, any goal is likely to have a tentative, provisional quality. Quite often, it is impossible to set goals that have a final or binding quality, but it is possible to proceed toward a general goal in a stepwise manner, with the goal gaining more definition as one moves toward it.

Planning

Given a statement of a goal, the second phase is planning the way to achieve it. Since goals are tentative, planning often has to take place more or less in the dark, particularly in the early stages of an operation before goals have become definitive and clear. Regardless of the conditions, however, planning must occur before a specific action step can be launched.

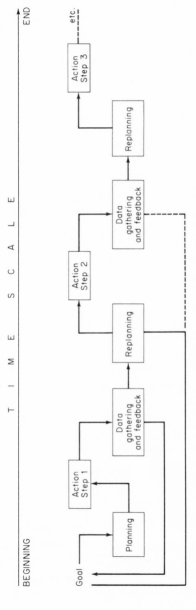

figure 1 *The use of action research as a critique method.* (From *Seminar on Strategies of Critique Materials*. Copyright © Scientific Methods, Inc., 1977)

First action step

The next phase is taking an action to move toward a goal. Given the goal and a plan for achieving it, action is required to get closer to it. In the diagram this is Action Step 1.

Data-gathering or feedback phase

Now comes the critical phase of data gathering and feedback. It provides steering information and is a measure by which to evaluate the progress made toward the goal, the adequacy of planning, and the quality and effectiveness of each given action step. By inserting feedback into the problem-solving process, it is possible to describe what progress is being made and whether it is real progress toward the goal. The critique step may demonstrate that the goal is unrealistic, the plan poor, or the action step unsuccessful. This is why it is important to measure whether or not progress is being made, and what kinds of feelings are being produced in the people affected by it.

Generalization

An element that is missing from the Action Research Model now needs to be introduced. It is generalization. After all elements in the model have been completed, it is desirable to identify any generalizations that offer insight into the whole activity or that provide clarification for better performance in future situations. Such generalizations may be concrete or action-oriented or they may deal with systematic concepts and principles. This is the critique step which makes it more fully possible to learn from experience, rather than simply using the Action Research Model for better management and problem solving.

Second action step

Given, first, the facts developed from data and other methods of evaluation and, second, a reexamination of the original goal to determine whether it needs to be modified or changed, new planning for the next action step is now possible.

The primary difference between action research and the other forms of critique is that it is a systematic way of using goal setting, along with involvement and commitment, to motivate effort. It is an *orderly* approach as contrasted with the impromptu critique of participant observation.

Action research may be used in any cycle of goal-achieving activity. Alternatively, the responsibility for conducting it may be shared with outsiders who become data gatherers and who assume responsibility for feeding data back into the system at needed points so progress evaluations can be made and replanning can take place. A variation of action research is that it need not necessarily be inserted at the beginning of a new cycle of performance to be useful. Any situation can be interrupted at any point to introduce action research critique. Thus, any individual or a group engaged in an activity that has a definable goal can introduce an action model at any time to reformulate the goal and, when this has been done, to plot steps for gathering data to assess how the activities are contributing toward attainment of the stated goal. The data can be used in a standard critique way to evaluate the adequacy of planning, organizing, staffing, controlling, or directing. Corrections calculated to move the operation toward its goals can then be applied through replanning.

There are numerous examples of how an Action Research Model may be used, and by doing so, a significant difference is created in how an activity occurs versus how it would normally be done. One of these examples involves accepting new products from a supplier under conditions where a warranty is involved. Consider the following. Shipbuilders routinely provide a warranty detailing the operating specifications they have built into a ship and the performance standards that the owner has a right to expect in sailing that ship. This is true not only for passenger ships but also for tankers, freighters, and even most pleasure craft.

The conventional practice of accepting a ship from its builder is for the captain to be designated, and then a crew is assembled. Before launching, the crew takes several days to become familiar with the ship's machinery and characteristics in its operation that can only be known through firsthand examination of how the ship has been put together and is expected to perform. The ship is then taken on a shakedown cruise to note all possible defects. The fact that a warranty specifies what the owner has a right to expect in terms of performance standards is forgotten, except when there is a gross malfunction. Gross malfunctions and significant departures from the warranty are reported to the captain. Many limitations in the ship are taken for granted, with the crew working around them as best it can.

To use an Action Research Design under these conditions, the captain would be appointed and the crew assembled, as in the conventional case. However, before boarding the ship, the crew would first become acquainted, individually and as a team, with the specifications for ship performance, machinery, and other sub-components written into the warranty. Then operating manuals specifying the proper operational approach to various pieces of equipment are consulted and critiqued for standard and unique features. Only at this point does the crew go aboard to learn the actual properties and equipment of the ship. The ship will be tested regarding its limits, both maximums and minimums, and its components and equipment, rather than limiting the shakedown to the average range. The next step is taking the ship to sea.

Four significant properties of an Action Research Model have been introduced up to this point. The first relates to clarification of performance goals expected from the ship as set out in the warranty. This becomes the ideal operating model. The second step is planning how the ship will be brought into service. The plan is to operate the ship according to warranty and operating manual specifications to the maximum degree possible. All deviations from specifications are to be noted and discrepancies between the actual operation of the ship and the warranty specifications are established. This becomes the actual or operating model.

The third step involves the actual data gathering and feedback of findings to a common source so there is a systematic and comprehensive basis for evaluating the ship's operating performance against the standards in the warranty and various operating manuals.

The final step is replanning. This entails, to whatever degree necessary, the ship's captain and crew joining with the shipbuilder or his representatives to solve problems that arose during the shakedown cruise.

This Action Research Model, then, provides a way of learning to operate the ship according to its specifications and of identifying discrepancies between what the owner has a right to expect and what in fact has been delivered. It also provides a basis for replanning the solution of these problems with the shipbuilder, who is to see that deficiencies are corrected before his responsibilities under the warranty have been completed.

Another example of action research is football. The goal of winning is clear at the beginning of a game. A game plan or strategy is developed and implemented. Planning, organizing, staffing, directing, and controlling strategies have already been worked out and are expected to be implemented as the game proceeds. However, because of the character of the game itself, some previously reached decisions may have to be changed as the situation develops. The half-time locker-room situation provides opportunities to critique what has happened in terms of progress toward the goal. Expert observers, TV, and so on, feed back to team members data pertinent to their understanding of the changes needed to increase the probability of success. The remaining part of the game can be considered as another activity cycle the coach uses for introducing further adjustments in the game plan.

A procedure useful for data gathering in action research and discrepancy models is called *survey research.* This is a more formalized way of asking individuals to react to the same situation so their reactions can be summarized in a quantitative manner. Usually, a large number of people are involved in completing a questionnaire. Statistical summaries are then used to feed data back for critique purposes so situations can be diagnosed, evaluated, and changed.

Goal Setting in Action Research

Goals useful in action research are set in a number of different ways. One question is, "By whom are they set?" Those who set the goals may not be involved in the implementation program for reaching them. In other words, goal setting (and planning) are separated from implementation. On the other hand, the same people who set goals and initiate plans may be those engaged in the implementation effort. All things being equal, it is better if those who set goals (and plan) also engage in achieving them.

An equally important, though different, issue is related to how goals are set. A common practice is for people to sit down and agree on what the goals might be in a more or less intuitive way. A better alternative is through a force field analysis, which is a passive way of goal setting that relies on changing certain parts of the situation in the hope that the overall result will improve. A force field analysis starts with examining what is actually happening in the situation.

Determining the actual through force field analysis

Any activity that has more or less standard level may be regarded as being in equilibrium. Equilibriums, or levels, are held in place by two kinds of forces. Force field analysis is a way of analyzing a situation of constant level activities to determine what actually is happening.[2] There are two kinds of forces exerted on a level: driving forces and restraining forces.

Driving forces constitute influences that tend to increase the rate of production. Pressure from the boss to work harder, desire for more pay in a piece rate situation, and a feeling of involvement and responsibility are driving forces.

Restraining forces are influences that tend to reduce the level of productivity. Fatigue, resentment of boss pressure, apathy, and indifference toward what happens are restraining forces. The level that exists for any activity is a result of driving and restraining forces coming into balance with one another. They are in equilibrium.

Here is an example of a force field analysis applied to a typical problem: the rate of production of tennis rackets. Figure 2 is organized into two time periods. Time 1 shows the force field as it existed at an initial point, and Time 2, after changes had been introduced.

Note that the arrows that push the level up are longer the farther away they are from the level. This means that a heavier influence is exerted by the length of the arrow. The same is true for the restraining forces. The arrows that identify factors of least influence

[2]Kurt Lewin, *Field Theory in Social Science* (New York: Harper, 1951), pp. 224–226

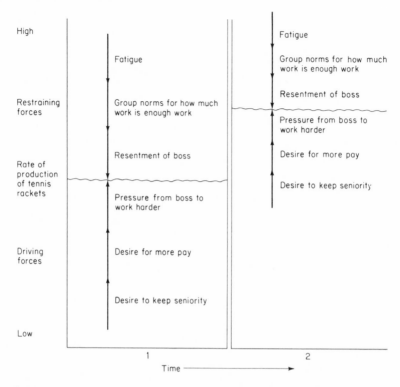

figure 2 *Forces operating in a production setting at Time 1 and after Critique Time 2.*

are shorter than those which identify factors of greatest influence.

An examination of Figure 2 shows that the kinds of forces that tend to increase the production rate are pressures from the boss to work harder, the desire for more pay, and the desire to keep seniority. On the other side of the level are the restraining forces: resentment of the boss; group norms for how much is enough work, that is, a fair day's work for a fair day's pay; and fatigue. Many other influences might be identified but these are typical of the kinds of forces that act on the one hand to push the level higher, and on the other, to prevent its going upward.

Time period 2, shown on the right-hand side of Figure 2, demonstrates that something has been done to change the force field. The actions taken have been to reduce restraining forces, and this is shown by the fact that now the degree of resentment felt toward the boss is significantly less, and the norms that govern output have become significantly less restrictive. Fatigue remains about the same. Without a shift in driving forces but with a reduction in restraining forces, an increment of productivity has been achieved.

The method used to gain improved understanding of the boss and to reduce resentment and the restrictive character of norms involved participant-observation kinds of discussion, in which members of the group evaluated their own feelings and attitudes. In this way, improved understanding resulted as to why they had kept productivity at the level that had become characteristic of the situation.

Thus, to change a level upward (frequency, volume, etc.), it is necessary to increase driving forces or reduce restraining forces, or both. The effort to shift a level upward that relies solely on increasing driving forces may only promote resistance to change, because the restraining forces remain as they were. The effort to shift a level upward that relies solely on reducing or removing restraining forces may be more successful. Then the level can "float" up, at least to some amount, if driving forces of sufficient magnitude are present, as was shown in Figure 2.

The same reasoning applies to shifting a level in a downward direction. In this instance, removing driving forces is likely to produce less resistance than increasing restraining forces. In either case, the optimal basis of shifting from one level to another is to change both restraining and driving forces, either simultaneously or successively.

Survey research

A procedure which is useful for data gathering in action research and discrepancy models is called survey research. This is a more formalized way of asking individuals to react to the same situation in such a way that their reactions can be summarized quantitatively. Usually, a larger number of people is involved in completing a questionnaire. Statistical summaries are then used to feed data back for critique purposes so situations can be diagnosed, evaluated, and changed.

Discrepancy Models

Four different discrepancy models are currently being used in the management field as the basis for learning from critique. They are (1) deviation from a preset standard, (2) obligation models, (3) ideal versus actual models, and (4) theory-based models.

Deviation from a preset standard

Kepner-Tregoe problem analysis[3] can be used by those in the situation in much the same way an inspector comes from the outside to locate deviations from a standard and make recommendations for how they might be dealt with.

In a problem analysis, a more or less standard series of steps is specified for determining what the problem is and what needs to be done to remedy it. The procedure is most applicable to studying performance and product results, though occasionally procedures might also be the focus of study. In any event, the starting point is to begin with the definition of an expected standard of performance or specifications for the product. If what is actually being achieved is not the same as the standard, the deviation is identified and its causes determined. Next, alternative ways of achieving the result are evaluated against the preset standards. The alternative which is most likely to achieve the desired performance or product according to the specifications is selected and tested for possible negative side effects. Other contingencies which might enter the situation are examined prior to making the final determination on which action steps should be taken.

Obligation models

An obligation model is used when the performance (i.e., product, procedure, etc.) desired is specified in concrete terms and deviations from it are sanctioned by legal or other forms of power. The model itself may be imposed on those who are expected to follow it. The obligation model has several advantages; for example, assuring uniformity; drawing attention to a problem that previously had been unrecognized; and attaining the desired action without use-

[3] Charles H. Kepner and Benjamin B. Tregoe, *The Rational Manager* (New York: McGraw-Hill, 1965).

less trial-and-error efforts, which result in poorer solutions than the one contained in the model.

Recent developments in the U.S. civil rights movement exemplify the use of an obligation model. Initiating action in a culture where the status quo had been unthinkingly accepted for such a long period of time that possible changes in it could not readily be seen was the issue. The continuation of "no action" was congruent with history, but in violation of the newly enacted legislation. The demand for affirmative action programs was the result.

These programs provide a way of ending such a stalemate. They also constitute an example of anticipatory critique by those responsible for a situation being called on to specify what they *intend* to do to bring current practices into accordance with the law which specifies the desired practice. Designing such plans compels a study of the present situation and identifying actions necessary to shift the situation from what it is to what it is expected to become. The affirmative action program is then submitted to authorities who evaluate whether it meets progress standards for reaching compliance. This is a second kind of learning. Those who design the program in the first place (i.e., the product) then get feedback on its acceptability from those responsible for enforcement. Execution of the program follows; if it is not acceptable, further inquiry is necessary to resubmit intended plans. During this step, monitoring (see Chapter 2) may be used as the basis for critique of implementation.

Though affirmative action programs originated as a way of inducing change to resolve race-related issues by bringing performance into compliance with law, obligation models are not restricted to that field of use. Corporate policy may be the basis for an obligation model. Say, for example, a corporation initiates a new policy with regard to a business code, the need for which has been repeatedly demonstrated, particularly by questionable dealings in multinational companies. Each segment of the corporation is asked to develop an action program which, when implemented, brings its conduct into congruence with corporate policy. Similar to affirmative action programs, monitoring may be used to evaluate progress and problems arising during the shiftover, and financial or other penalties and rewards relied on for additional "pressure" to ensure conduct is in line with the agreed-on action program.

Once agreed on, the action program operates to induce change. It is an example of a discrepancy model of problem solving. A set of conditions or standards is mandated. The impetus to change is provided by the recognition of an unacceptable past or present status compared to the mandate of what will be acceptable. This is an example of strategic assessment which focuses learning on processes and procedures, first, for the purpose of planning and, thereafter, for purposes of control.

In contrast with corporate policy at the organization level, behavior modeling is an approach to learning from experience that focuses on solving problems that people have in dealing with others, particularly in a supervisory/subordinate relationship.[4] These may include reducing absenteeism, teaching an employee a new task, or handling employees' complaints. In this approach, a standard way to solve the problem is presented as the model of a workable approach. Next, participants practice applying the model. The goal is to replicate the key behaviorial aspects of the model in their own actions. They receive feedback as to how well their behavior matches the model from other participants as well as the program administrator. The purpose is to reduce discrepancies between a person's actual behavior and that called for by the model. Later, in on-the-job applications of the model, participants are given feedback by the boss regarding their effectiveness in applying the model. This use of behavior modeling is a combination of the discrepancy approach and inspection, since both program administrators and participant bosses are "experts," who aid the participants in determining how well their personal behavior fits that called for in terms of a model they have been presented with.

Ideal versus actual models

The ideal-versus-actual strategy of critique engages those involved in reaching agreement on what the ideal circumstances would be were they unfettered by traditions, precedents, and past practices, or by prior difficulties in planning, organizing, staffing, directing, and controlling. Unlike the obligation model, the ideal is usually

---

[4]William Byham and James Robinson, "Interaction Modeling: A New Concept in Supervisory Training," *Training and Development Journal,* 30 (2): 20–33, 1976.

established by those in charge of the activity. Actual practice is also studied by those who "own" the problem to identify discrepancies.

Sometimes individuals know what is ideal in the sense that they have many times observed what *should* be happening. As with other discrepancy models, once an ideal model has been formulated and contrasted with actual practice, it becomes possible to diagnose, evaluate, generalize, interpret, and, finally, plan the steps essential for moving away from actual practice in the direction of the ideal model.

Putting the ideal and actual discrepancy models into practice in one company resulted in reducing by half the downtime due to industrial relations problems. The statement of actual industrial relations practice when the model was being constructed read, "This company awaits union pressures in respect to changes in wages, conditions, demarcation issues, etc. and responds to them by discussion, negotiation, and bargaining when they are applied. The goal is to give away as little as possible." This contrasted with the statement of the ideal policy—"To work actively with the union in respect to current and future issues which are of mutual interest to the union, employees, and the company." Putting the new statement to work yielded the results described and left this particular company in a stronger position to exercise initiative than it had at any previous time been able to achieve.

Theory-based models

A theory-based model is used as a critique basis whenever those involved in an experience employ behavioral science principles as the basis for contrasting actual circumstances with a theoretical model. Three widely known, theory-based, ideal-actual models are Theory X and Theory Y, System 4, and the Managerial Grid.

Two models of management are represented in Theory X and Theory Y. In the Theory X model managers exercise authority to ensure that work is carried out obediently by subordinates. This then becomes the basis for achieving productivity. Theory Y is premised on collaborative endeavor between managers and subordinates to achieve the same purpose, namely, productivity. In applying the theory-based model of critique, managers study Theories X and Y as two systematic descriptions of behavior alternatives. Once each is understood, it is possible for managers to evaluate their own actual situation to determine the extent to which it approximates the assumptions contained in Theory X, as contrasted with those in Theory Y. Once the theory-versus-practice analysis has been completed, causes for the differences are identified. Implications for changes are drawn and participants plan how they can move in the directions they regard as desirable.

A set of scales based on Theory X and Theory Y concepts is shown below.[5] The left side of each scale represents X, the right Y.

	X					Y	
	High suspicion					High trust	
Trust	1	2	3	4	5	6	7
	Every one for oneself					Genuine concern for each other	
Support	1	2	3	4	5	6	7
	Guarded, cautious					Open and honest	
Communication	1	2	3	4	5	6	7
	We don't listen to each other					We understand and are understood	
Listening	1	2	3	4	5	6	7
	Not understood					Clearly understood	
Team objectives	1	2	3	4	5	6	7
	Denied, avoided					Accepted as inevitable and desirable, and worked through	
Conflict	1	2	3	4	5	6	7

For critiquing a group process, members rate their team on these seven-point scales. Then the team as a whole discusses the situa-

[5] Douglas McGregor, *The Human Side of Enterprise* (New York: McGraw-Hill, 1960).

tion indicated by average scores for any item rating less than five and for those scales which show a wide range of individual ratings. Team members are asked to consider and identify the "why" of the situations as they have pictured them.

One of the advantages of such a set of theory-based scales is that a team can use it to deal with issues that it might not otherwise recognize as being important. For example, the sample set above includes questions concerned with mutual trust and support, communication, listening, team objectives, and conflict. Though these are known to be significant factors which have a bearing on team effectiveness, most are not problems that managers spontaneously raise in daily work meetings in such clear-cut and undisguised terms. When they are identified in this way, team members can plan corrective steps to increase the effectiveness of their team process whenever they think an improvement is needed.

System 4 combines a research-based set of theories with survey research data gathering as previously described.[6] System 4 concepts are organized according to four classes of action described as autocracy, benevolent autocracy, consultative, and participative management. Questionnaires include items which permit an evaluation to be made of the extent management is being practiced according to each of these four methods of supervision. They provide raw data which participants use to evaluate what their actual here-and-now management practices are. They can then determine whether changes are needed to move into a System 4 basis of management.

A third theory-versus-practice model is the Managerial Grid.[7] This approach identifies thirteen theories of management, five of which are of primary importance in everyday practice. The theories are:

9,1   Authority-obedience as the basis of control.

1,9   Approximates the conditions of permissive leadership where only the mildest and most inoffensive supervision is offered.

1,1   An abandonment of responsibility on a "let it drift" basis.

5,5   Organization-person dynamics, with supervision based on the

---

[6]Rensis Likert, *The Human Organization* (New York: McGraw-Hill, 1967).

[7]Robert R. Blake and Jane Srygley Mouton, *The New Managerial Grid* (Houston: Gulf Publishing Co., 1978).

leader not asking for more or different actions from those managed than past experience has led people to expect.

9,9 Premised on setting clear and challenging goals and then creating sound conditions of teamwork which ensure that such goals are realized. When conflicts arise as to the best procedures for accomplishing goals, they are resolved by 9,9 confrontation of differences, rather than by 9,1 suppression, 1,9 smoothing, 1,1 neutrality, or 5,5 compromise.

Using the Managerial Grid as a discrepancy model, managers study these theories and reach agreement as to which is most suited to their situation. They then study actual management practices as they have been experienced and determine which theory or what combination of theories they typify. With discrepancies thus identified, diagnosis is possible as the basis for the generalization, interpretation, and planning steps necessary for changing from their actual practices toward the theories which create more effective management and higher quality outcomes and results.

These three theory-based, ideal-actual model approaches are among the more widely known and used examples of basic strategies for inducing change. However, regardless of the theory used, this approach encounters a difficulty arising from self-deception. Participants often see themselves and their performance to be better than they are and differently from the way they are viewed by others. Self-deception is a barrier to use of the theory-versus-practice model. To overcome it, participants must learn the conditions under which self-deception can be eliminated so that their own situation can be observed more realistically as a basis for planning steps to strengthen their own effectiveness.

A relatively new approach for learning from experience is referred to as zero-based budgeting. It is pertinent for use whenever traditions, precedents, and past practices need fundamental reexamination and testing, rather than acceptance at face value. This strategy begins with the assumption that anything done in the past no longer will be funded unless circumstances justify its continuation. As a result, those activities currently funded have to be studied and evaluated in order to determine whether their continuance is justified, and if so, to what degree.

Study and evaluation of past experience and decision in the light of evidence is the newly introduced step that is not required in standard or conventional approaches to budgeting. The model against which past performance is evaluated is referred to as the "null hypothesis," which means that nothing from the past is justified in its own right. Therefore, unless present and future justifications for its continuation can be demonstrated, the past performance may be eliminated. The weakness of this model is that it offers no criteria for evaluating the appropriateness of continuation; as a result, defensiveness, rationalization, and other justifications may be relied on to protect sacred cows, white elephants, and other projects when sole justification is vested interest.

An advantage of zero-based budgeting over conventional methods is that older projects are put on an equal footing with new ones, and all get equal scrutiny. Only new projects get that kind of study in classical approaches to budgeting.

How to Conduct an Ideal-Actual
Strategic Assessment

The ideal-actual strategic assessment method is described in the following steps. The reader will see pertinent differences between this method and the alternative methods already described.

Participation in the formulation of an ideal model usually is limited to individuals or organization members whose knowledge, experience, background, and competence qualify them as expert in the topic to be evaluated. The boss or leader reviews with key members the wisdom of designing an ideal model based on consensus among those who can contribute to its formulation. Procedural leadership is offered by the administrative head (the boss or leader) or it shifts according to the particular topic being discussed. Certain participants are likely to have specialist knowledge in some topics and can therefore see the ramifications of exploring a particular issue.

In dealing with reservations and doubts, experts, because they are more likely to see complexity, are more likely to get themselves involved in disagreements than less knowledgeable people, who see fewer implications given the same problem. When experts disagree, far more significance should be attached to resolving the conflict by confrontation and the use of data and logic than when disagreement arises among persons who are not so knowledgeable. The boss or leader takes initiative to ensure that such conflicts are confronted and resolved rather than allowing resolution to be based on arbitration or compromise.

Agreements reached as to the ideal model are submitted not only to expert consensus but are recorded on a step-by-step basis. This means that as agreement is reached, it is expressed in written, linear sentence and paragraph texts so that it can later be reviewed and revised.

The boss or leader takes whatever steps are necessary to ensure that the ideal modeling is not marred by the introduction of modification based on traditions or past practice. Actions that can only be taken when new knowledge or new technology has been developed *cannot* form part of an ideal model. The steps required to acquire the needed knowledge or technology *can* form a part of the model.

The activity starts by specifying the ideal model and proceeds by analyzing actual practice as the basis of diagnosis. This sequence is important and should not be reversed. It is necessary because once an ideal formulation has been developed, the sequence provides an analytical framework for more objectivity in seeing what actual practices and standards are. The reverse sequence eliminates this possibility.

The steps above should be repeated in formulating a description of the actual situation. Care should be taken to avoid rationalizing what is going on in the situation. This means two things. The first is the tendency to see what is as what it should be. Creating an ideal model as a first step prevents this kind of rationalization. The second is that participants should avoid describing the actual situation more favorably than it really is. One way of guarding against this is to require participants to provide examples that support their statements about the actual circumstances. This use of examples provides objective evidence. This step is important because if the actual seems to be better than it really is, then motivation to change and improve is lessened. On the other hand, real change may not be achieved because the gap between ideal and actual, being larger than was realized, has not been bridged.

Each topic in the ideal model is placed in a priority or sequential order, the first being the issue most needing attention, the second being the next issue most needing attention, and so on. The descriptions of actual practice are then aligned to correspond with the issues in the ideal model.

When an issue present in the ideal model was not touched on in describing the actual, the boss or leader initiates a discussion to fill this gap. When a condition touched on in the description of the actual does not have a matching specification in the ideal strategic model, the boss or leader takes the steps necessary to fill this omission.

A comparison, specification by specification, is made between the ideal and actual model. This comparison leads to the identification of deficiencies in actual performance that are capable of specific improvement or change. Impracticalities in the strategic model (e.g., changes that are unattainable because of fixed constraints relating to personnel, financial resources, and the like) are also identified.

The diagnosis of deficiencies in the actual model is reviewed to ensure consensus among all the generalists and expert managers who are involved in it, affected by it, or have to implement it.

Issues needing change are placed in priority representing:

■ Practicality of change from a time perspective, those most subject to change in the immediate present being placed first

■ Those most important, with the importance criterion being judged against standards of effectiveness, and those changes which would make the maximum contribution to effectiveness being placed in highest priority

■ A resolution of contradictions between time feasibility and effectiveness criteria in favor of the requirement for effectiveness

In implementing the change plan involving review, critique, and replanning, specific agreements are reached as to the actions to be taken. This also includes the persons to be responsible for taking actions, the time in which these actions are to be taken and completed, and reporting arrangements to ensure that roadblocks are eliminated and coordination is maintained. The use of strategic assessment is complete only when the design experts have reconvened to review progress, to critique weaknesses of the plan as seen at that point in time, and to replan for those changes either in direction or pace that can be anticipated.

Communicating the strategic model and the plan of action is an important part of implementation. A sound way to communicate conclusions reached is to create a learning exercise using the contents of the ideal and actual descriptions in a team effectiveness design.[8] Participants should include all persons who might be able to contribute to the strengthening of the model or the plan of action to implement it, those who will be engaged in its implementation, and those who will have responsibility for its evaluation. Conclusions reached by personnel involved in the total change effort but who are not the design experts should be communicated to the design experts for review and evaluation to ensure that weight is given to and use is made of their contributions.

Strengths and Limitations

Strategic assessment is useful when:

- Problems arise, whether they are subject to solution by systematic as contrasted to pragmatic or eclectic approaches.
- A sufficient outline exists of what the real problem is to permit the formulation of a goal.
- A proactive rather than reactive posture is taken toward solving the problem.
- There is a natural tie between planning and activities, that is, plans influence activities which, in turn, influence the plans.
- People are available with sufficient expertise to ensure the possibility of synergy.
- A shift in basic direction is needed.
- A way of measuring progress is needed.
- Willingness to be open and critical of what is being done is present.

Strategic assessment is not useful when:

- Those responsible for activities do not have a sufficient degree of expertise to be able to make fundamental judgments.
- Designing the ideal model is not done by those responsible for implementing it.

---

[8] Jane Srygley Mouton and Robert R. Blake, *Instrumented Team Learning: A Behavioral Approach to Student-Centered Learning* (Austin, Tex.: Scientific Methods, Inc., 1975).

■ It is impractical or impossible to describe a situation in terms of systematic variables.

■ The culture of the firm or situation is such that an evolutionary as opposed to a systematic stance is the operating value system.

■ A basic mechanism is needed to evaluate whether a shift of direction is needed.

■ Complacency has resulted in personnel becoming accustomed to the situation without thinking about it in a critical, though constructive, manner.

Strategic assessment, in other words, is a way of planning for the future and learning to implement plans in the here and now. It is most useful when those responsible for activities are also responsible for changing the direction of their activities.

Summary

Strategic methods of assessment are among the most useful approaches to critique. They have the distinct advantage of allowing those involved to imagine alternative possibilities to what they are currently doing. In this way, they see the status quo in the light of new possibilities rather than simply examining situations for how to improve the here-and-now circumstances.

SIX

Conditions for
Effective Use
of Critique

Critique relies on those who are responsible for a situation to bring about change. If critique is to be effective, however, certain requirements must be met. This chapter describes some of those requirements.

Climate

One significant feature that can contribute to or detract from the effectiveness of critique is the climate within the situation. Climates that are hostile or win/lose, soft and supportive, or compromising can cause uninformative answers to be obtained from even the best-formulated critique strategy. By contrast, an open, straight-forward climate can result in effective application of critique.

The properties of a climate that are unfavorable for effective learning from experience, Model 1, in contrast with a more favorable climate, Model 2, have been described by Argyris and Schön.[1] There are four assumptions underlying participants' behavior in Model 1 that detract from effective critique.

[1] Chris Argyris and Donald Schön, *Theory in Practice: Increasing Professional Effectiveness* (San Francisco: Jossey-Bass, 1974).

In Model 1, each participant:
- Seeks to achieve private purposes.
- Is oriented to win.
- Suppresses negative feelings and attitudes by minimizing the opportunity of others' expressing them.
- Emphasizes rationality ("we need to be rational and logical about this . . .") as opposed to the open expression of logical contradictions and emotional ambivalences.

The basic value supported by the assumptions underlying Model 1 is the exercise of control and mastery over people, events, and conditions. One way for individuals with such values to do this is to put themselves in a position with the "authority" to define what *is* valid information. For example, ". . . If A tells B that B's performance is ineffective and if A also decides what *is* ineffective and refuses to let B have any influence over the criteria, then B will feel highly controlled. Similarly, if A tells B that B is defensive or manipulative and, again, decides on the validity of these attributes, then B will feel highly controlled."[2]

What are the consequences? ". . . they tend to produce defensiveness and closedness in people because unilateral control does not tend to produce valid feedback." Thus the above assumptions are adverse to a climate essential for critique learning. In addition, they lead to contradictory behavior.

The authoritarian, autocratic climate pictured in Model 1 (the 9, 1 position on the Blake and Mouton Managerial Grid) makes it unlikely that critique strategies will be based on voluntary, open collaboration in a straightforward way. Data, opinions, and attitudes voiced are likely to be circumspect, noninformative, and relate only to noncontroversial elements in the situation under review.

Some other styles also are adverse, in their own different ways, to the encouragement of critique. A "supportive" climate (1, 9 on the Managerial Grid) is restrictive because its norms reinforce complimentary feedback but fail to confront the negative aspects of behavior. A 1, 1 Managerial Grid climate of indifference is unlikely to promote critique because the motivation to learn is absent. A 5, 5

---

[2] Ibid.

Grid climate of shallow compromise, in which the definition of legitimate data is modified in the light of the need for acceptability, distorts critique processes by hiding things that need to be examined, instead of bringing them into the open.

One solution is to reverse these values. This is possible by creating a climate in which there is:

■ A consensus-based definition of purpose, that is, commitment to decisions made.

■ A problem-solving rather than a win/lose orientation.

■ Openness to both negative and positive feelings and attitudes.

■ Respect for emotions in feedback, as well as for irrational formulations that need to be sorted out and clarified.

These four values mirror the basic 9,9 Managerial Grid assumptions.[3] They lead to the conclusion that participants who expect to utilize critique need to develop, in advance, agreed-on norms and values that can support their critique activities. Norms and values that need to be developed to reach personal commitment on their use can be formulated by seeking answers to the following questions.

■ In undertaking to use critique, is it our purpose to facilitate immediate problem solving as well as to learn from the experience?

■ Are participants trying to win their points of view, or to solve the real problem?

■ Is it legitimate for participants to express negative emotions if they feel them, for release or as informative feedback?

■ Is the discussion limited to rational arguments, or are emotions and feelings about problems and reservations and doubts brought into the open?

■ Do we consider the validity of the approach to the problem or the capacity of participants to solve it, or both, to be legitimate issues for discussion?

Resolution of these issues is difficult until participants have learned to reject indifferent, supportive, authoritarian, and shallow compromise assumptions and have acquired the skill for operating in 9, 9 Grid teamwork ways.

[3]Robert R. Blake and Jane Srygley Mouton, *Corporate Excellence Through Grid Organization Development* (Houston: Gulf Publishing Co., 1968).

Even though inspection may be the only practical means of data gathering, it is probably closer to 9, 1 Grid assumptions than is the case with other critique methods. It has an inherent premise of suspicion and distrust on the part of the inspector whose job is to verify the product or performance of others. Simulation usually emphasizes impersonal aspects of performance, products, or procedures. Unless applied on a very personal basis, simulations do not create climate problems. A climate of the 9, 9 Grid variety, which includes skills of asking questions and listening, is indispensable to the effective use of participant observation or strategic assessment.

Anonymity versus Identification of the Feedback Source

One dilemma frequently posed, particularly with respect to feedback regarding process or people, is the issue of anonymity versus identification of the source of feedback. The argument for anonymity is that when the climate is not conducive to candor and openness, more accurate data are likely to be obtained. Yet a significant kind of information is potentially lost without identification. When others know "who thinks what," then further information can be elicited, a differential weighting can be given to different people's views, or valid data found to be lacking may be added. Probably the soundest condition is one where the climate essential for openness is present and anonymity has no place on people's lists of needs.

Data-gathering Skills

Though a good climate is essential for maximizing learning from experience, it is insufficient if participants lack certain data-gathering skills, such as asking questions and active listening.

Asking questions

Skill in posing questions that prompt participants to reveal important data and attitudes is important for several reasons. First, by formulating questions in a sound way, the questioner can gain insight into how respondents think. Second, respondents gain increased insight into their own thinking. Third, respondents are enabled to contribute more fully by sharing personal insights with others. Finally, a well-posed question does not compel the respondents to tell more than they wish to reveal.

What are the properties or characteristics of a sound question? Other things being equal, a sound question:

■ Does not commit a respondent to one or another side of a discussion on a "yes, I agree," or "no, I disagree" basis.

■ Is left open-ended rather than suggesting an answer, for example, "How did you feel when X happened?" is better than, "Did you feel tense when X happened?"

■ Invites description rather than evaluation, and a response, "This is what I was thinking," rather than, "I disliked that remark."

■ Invites an answer expressed as an "I message," so that the respondent emphasizes personal thoughts and feelings, that is, "This is my reaction . . ." rather than perceptions or inferences regarding the reactions of others, for example, "Here's what you seemed to be thinking."

■ Communicates that the reactions of the respondent are respected. "I would like to understand your reactions to X" is better than, "Now it's your turn to report."

These kinds of questions, together with active listening, increase the likelihood that critique will produce real learning.

Active listening

Another data-gathering skill is active listening. Since a key aspect of critique is the valid interpretation of others' experiences, learning to listen is important. What is said is only as informative as the listener permits it to be. Accurate listening does not occur if biases, prejudices, preconceptions, preoccupations, or win/lose attitudes interfere with the speaker. Valid listening, in other words, happens only when what the listener thinks the speaker said conforms with what the speaker intended to convey. This does not mean that what the speaker says is devoid of biases, prejudices, preconceptions, preoccupations, or win/lose attitudes. It means that the listener "hears" these themes according to the speaker's self-understanding of what is said. The listener may or may not accept them or agree with them, but they are understood.

How is it possible to learn to achieve this degree of active listening? Guidelines to some of the things that one can do to become an active listener include the following points:[4]

1. Try to understand the speaker's own point of view, though you may not accept that point of view as valid for problem solving. This may mean restating what the speaker said to ensure correct interpretation, for example, "This is what I hear you saying . . ."

2. Encourage the speaker to talk more, that is, look the person in the eye, smile, nod understanding, say, "uh-huh."

3. Help and encourage the speaker to talk about how the situation is seen from the speaker's viewpoint through the use of "tell me more" expressions.

4. Clarify your own understanding of the speaker's feelings by asking, for example, "Is this how you feel . . .?"

Another strategy is to critique the quality of listening on a continuing basis. Then distortions can be identified and brought to a listener's attention to increase awareness. Once several examples are available, it is possible for the listener to review them for common or characteristic themes. For example, when challenged, some people become more accurate in their listening. Others seem unable to improve, in which case a participant can "rehearse" understandings whenever listening pressures are suspected. These approaches, in other words, can be used to anticipate and thereby avoid falling repeatedly into the same mistakes.

Giving Personal Feedback without Arousing Defensiveness or Injuring Feelings

Learning from experience is most difficult under conditions where the limitations and deficiencies of individuals themselves are the cause of poor performance, process, and so on. Yet these people problems need to be dealt with so limitations and deficiencies can be replaced with skills and competence. A number of ways have been experimented with for making feedback more acceptable in the sense that another person can hear and accept it, and therefore make use of it without suffering feelings of personal injury.

One way is to give the feedback from nonevaluative perspectives. An evaluative statement is, "You should not have done that be-

[4]Robert R. Blake and Jane S. Mouton, *Consultation* (Reading, Mass.: Addison-Wesley, 1976).

cause. . . ." A nonevaluative statement is, "When you did that, this is the feeling that was going on inside me." In the latter case, the participant is not being evaluated, but given information about the reactions experienced. Self-judgment about whether to attempt to change is thus fostered.

Another approach accepts the inevitability of evaluations, but tries to shift them away from *moral* judgments, or judgments involving acceptance or rejection, toward the prediction and assessment of consequences. The participant giving the critique describes what has been observed, but also tries to specify what the consequences would be if the same behavior were continued or changed in various ways.

Another way to make personal critique more acceptable is to ensure that what is being critiqued is "alive" in the here-and-now sense. Experiences occurring on a moment-to-moment basis are easier to comprehend and react to objectively. Though one may still learn from past experiences, they are more difficult to reconstruct. Critique of here and now has more impact than critique of past happenings. Another strategy is to aid people to establish agreed-on norms regarding the way feedback is to be given and what kinds of behavior are appropriate for discussion. One set of rules most people can agree on and use is described in terms of "clean" as contrasted with "dirty" feedback. [5]

Dirty Feedback	*Clean Feedback*
Feelings expressed are insincere.	Open, clear display of authentic feelings and concern.
The statements are designed to hurt or injure the person being described.	The person being described can "take" the statements made about that individual.
The person being described is blamed for whatever happened ("themism").	The person making the statement feels responsible for what he or she may have contributed to the situation.
Humor is used sarcastically or to put down the other person.	
Vague, general, and judgmental statements are made.	Humor produces relaxation or relief.
Irrelevant behavior or past actions are recounted.	Specific concrete actions are described.
	Here-and-now behavior is described.

[5]George R. Bach and Peter Wyden, *The Intimate Enemy: How to Fight Fair in Love and Marriage* (New York: Avon Books, 1970).

Barriers to Effective Critique

The effective use of critique, particularly when the methods used include participation observation or strategic assessment, can be strengthened when those involved discuss and agree on the importance of reducing the barriers that exist.[6] Awareness of what these barriers are adds to the possibility that they can be reduced or even eliminated altogether. They are as follows:

■ Participants may become so involved in the content of problem solving that they are blinded to the need for checking out the soundness of what is going on.

■ Fear of failure or of wasting effort is sometimes the unstated reason for not stopping to critique. It is frequently also unreal.

■ The boss of a team needs to recognize whether strong personal convictions about what needs to be done block critique.

■ The boss has already decided the way things should go and believes critique will prevent the action from being taken.

■ The time consumed in carrying out critique may be more than can be justified from the gains that might be realized from using it.

■ There may be concern that if participants say what they really think, tempers will flare and frank expressions will cause the situation to get out of control.

■ Critique may show that the course of action being followed is wrong, but it may not reveal a better way. The fear is that the situation may end up in despair.

■ If negative interpersonal feelings are expressed, antagonisms can be inflamed that might lead to mutual destructiveness.

■ Members may be distrustful of one another to such a degree that no one is willing to give another an advantage by exposing what he or she thinks to criticism.

■ Members may screen what they are about to say for acceptability, before saying it. This may create the *appearance* of frankness, but the candor needed for bringing negative performance into the open will not occur.

[6]Robert R. Blake and Jane Srygley Mouton, *Corporate Excellence,* 1968.

Themism

All the above are more or less commonsense realities as to why the use of critique is less effective than it should be as an approach to learning from experience. One of the most important barriers occurs when people disown a problem even though they might be able to solve it. The problem belongs to someone else or to no one, but it is not theirs. Having no feeling of "ownership" for a problem, the person feels little responsibility for taking the necessary steps to deal with it. Solutions to be implemented remain unidentified.

Themism stands for all the variations of putting the responsibility elsewhere when, in point of fact, it would be healthier to take the responsibility oneself. Included are him (the boss), her (the wife), it (the company or the university), them (regulations, bureaucrats, the government, etc.). For convenience, themism stands for all these, because the same motivations appear to operate, regardless of the "target."

Themism masquerades under many rationalizations. Here are a few:

- "I can't do it if they never give me enough time" (or people, or equipment, etc.).
- "We've never done it like that before. They'd raise hell before they would approve it."
- "What they suggest sounds OK, but our situation is different."
- "That kind of thing won't work in our kind of business."

Any one of these rationalizations might be a valid reason for not exercising initiative. More often than not they are coverups a person uses to avoid the risk of failure and criticism for trying something new. Even when a risk exists in exercising initiative, it is unlikely to be great, and the fact that "it is easier to ask forgiveness than permission" reduces whatever risk there is even further. By comparison, the gains from taking initiative are great, not only for possible problem solving but also for personal satisfaction.

Shifting ownership of problems onto others rather than accepting responsibility for finding solutions is a very widespread phenomenon. Denial of personal responsibility through rationalization, justification, or repudiation of the entire situation has become rather commonplace.

To describe this attitude, however, is different than explaining how the ownership dilemma operates. If we can gain understanding of the dynamics of this attitude, it is possible that the use of critique to enable those who want to learn to solve their problems can be enhanced.

From psychoanalysis to organization development, the basic issue of personal resistance to accepting responsibility for problem solving is the same. Psychoanalysis is a good example, to make the point at one end of the spectrum. Since it is remote from most people's experiences, psychoanalysis provides a basis of analysis that can be looked at without the bias from personal involvement. In psychoanalysis the sequence of experiences of the client can be described as follows. The client feels ill in various ways, or others see that help is needed. The client eventually goes to a psychoanalyst and unloads the problems. All of a sudden the burden is lifted; the client feels better, freer. That is an almost universal reaction. Is it because the client unloaded the problems on the psychoanalyst; or if not, what is it related to? It is not so much that the client described the problems and felt a sense of release, but rather that the problem now belongs to somebody else; the psychoanalyst owns it. The client can feel relieved. Something positive has been done. This transfer of responsibility is followed by a period of romance, with the client feeling the psychoanalyst could not be more insightful, incisive, helpful, affectionate, warm; in short, a good person.

Time goes on. The client expects the help that had been anticipated, but it is not forthcoming. Eventually, uneasiness and unhappiness set in. The client now feels as much hatred toward the analyst as there was love previously. The therapist is no damn good. The client recognizes, "I've got my same problems. Every clue was given to what my problems are but I haven't received any help, so here I am. I was trusting, but this analyst is not trustworthy."

In a successful psychoanalysis, the patient comes to a third step beyond love and hate. The client's thoughts go something like this: "The therapist can't really help me to solve my own problems. The only solution to my problems is for me to help myself." The client has broken the resistance-to-change barrier. Now the psychoanalyst can be really helpful. By aiding the client to take the responsibility, the client comes to understand why those loving, then hateful, feelings occurred. Soon the client has learned about the feelings toward authority—too much affection when it looks helpful and supportive and too much rejection when it's not as helpful as had been hoped. Therefore, the real problem is in the client's own attitudes toward authority and the readiness to blame others, rather than accepting personal responsibility. By taking the initiative and becoming relieved of both dependence on and resentment toward authority, the client has become more responsible.

Early sensitivity training is another example. It was important in the 1950s and 60s, but is somewhat less popular today. At the beginning of a T-Group, people assemble around tables. A "trainer" is present whom everyone is "happy" to see; and everybody is happy to see everyone. There is anticipation and enthusiasm for the wonderful "miracles" that will occur. The implicit assumption is that the trainer, the person assigned responsibility for the group, will announce a discussion or activity agenda. With insight as to what is really going on, the trainer will enable members to learn a great deal.

This is a very deep-lying, though unrecognized, dependence on the trainer—the designated authority. The trainer does not do what others expect. The group flounders and nothing is done. The wonderful initial positive feelings for this fine, intelligent trainer turn into, "We're in trouble. The trainer is no damn good, and doesn't know what's going on. We ask questions and we get no answers. What are we doing here? We are probably wasting our time. We ought to pack and leave."

Eventually, though, someone is likely to say, "That's copping out. Leaving won't solve our problem. We haven't grappled with whatever our underlying difficulty is. Why can't we be effective? Let us ignore the trainer and take responsibility for ourselves. Let's find out what's going on. We can reason out what to do ourselves if the trainer can't tell us what to do."

Now the authority of the trainer has been rejected. The responsibility for solving the problem has been taken by the group. The group begins to move. People are involved; they are responsible for themselves. The trainer can now be helpful by being listened to, not as an authority whose word is final and complete, but as a voice of acknowledged competence. The shift is from dependence to counter-dependence to interdependent, shared responsibility for problem solving.

We see one key factor in resistance to change in these examples. It is the initial refusal of people to take ownership of problems on themselves until circumstances force them to do so. To take ownership means to concentrate personal effort, to make commitments, and to take risks by being responsible for problem solving. It is personal responsibility to try to do what may be difficult to do, even though failure may result. The entire situation can be avoided by a mental trick that says, "The problem is *theirs,* not mine." That is themism.

Only when this fundamental source of resistance to learning is reduced or eliminated is it likely that effective use can be made of critique for problem solving. The reason is that if people feel a problem is owned by someone else, they are not inclined to use problem-solving tools to resolve it on their own initiative. Evidence of such resistance may be experienced by the reader who says, ". . . that may apply to sick people, but I'm not sick," or, "That may explain a sensitivity group, but my problems are real life, not something way out."

No less damaging to learning is that the same attitude is also revealed in a different, almost opposite, way. The dynamic can be seen in the following. Appearing before a judge in a popular TV skit, a comedian absolves himself of all responsibility for his actions, saying, "The devil made me do it." This is another version of themism. They (the devil and his cousins) control the action, therefore the actor is not to be held accountable for his conduct.

This attitude is basic to understanding the reactions of many of the Watergate actors. For them, it was "the system that made me do it"; therefore they were not responsible. Equally so, it is basic to understanding the endless range of examples of unsound conduct and failure to critique it from CIA, FBI, and corporation officials who authorized or "winked" at payoffs for contracts in the 1965–1975 era. Themism makes it possible to engage in questionable activities by putting responsibility on others, rather than testing the actions against standards of excellence. Obviously, no learning is possible when this version of themism prevails.

Resistance to critique in everyday problem solving emanates from the very same attitudes as those described above. Can it be changed? Recognition of this resistance is sometimes sufficient to reduce or eliminate it. When deference or defiance of authority is extremely high, it may be necessary to employ additional strategies for reducing resistances. How can people be encouraged to increase their feelings of personal responsibility and therefore solve problems rather than blame other agencies and leave conflicts unsolved? One of the best ways is to understand the psychoanalysis, that is, the motivations for themism, as recounted here. Additional influences that cause people to become more aware of the depth of their own themisms through laboratory learning are possible, but these are beyond the scope of this study.

Origins of Themism

The beginnings of themism are found in the nursery, where everything is done for the child by parents and others who feel responsible for the child's well-being at a time when all the infant can do is signal distress or happiness. Patterns established in the nursery are continued. Many parents go on solving problems for their children or guide them in subtle ways which shifts responsibility for the children's problem solving and decision making off their shoulders. Often, when a child does exercise self-initiative, the result is failure and punishment, which increases reliance on *them,* the parents.

Grade school teachers pick up the same pattern when a child enters school and foster its development by teacher-tell education that rewards or punishes a child according to compliance with *them.* The problem is reinforced in college and in initial employment. Thus, the dynamics of themism are set at an early age and reinforced into maturity. Some child-rearing methods avoid themism by fostering self-responsibility at an early age and reinforcing independence as the child develops greater and greater skill. Even here, themism is present, though it may be very much less and easier to resolve entirely as a person enters adulthood and employment.

There is another angle. Involved is the boss, for example, who complains to a colleague about a subordinate but takes no action to confront or help the subordinate to change. Complaining may continue, but no change results. It must be accepted that the complaining contributes something to relieving the boss, who, at a deeper level, may avoid confronting the problem because "it would not do any good," the equivalent of putting the solution to the problem on the subordinate in contrast with exercising the kind of initiative that might solve it. Passivity persists; so does the problem.

A third source of themism is in the area of social and economic deprivation. Young people see the advantages enjoyed by others in comparison with their own relatively unfavorable circumstances. Others have the edge, sometimes a big one, at least in relative terms. The deprived feel disadvantaged, weak, and unable to compete, for the deprivation is no fault of their own. To see what others can do and to feel one's own inadequacy focuses in on *them.* It is but a short step to see problems as also belonging to and caused by *them,* and so shrug off responsibility for problem solving.

Sometimes passivity turns into antagonism and revenge against the "system." Then a person fights the system, seeking to "beat it" or strike back to redress the imbalance, as in theft, and sometimes to destroy it, for example, the burning of ghettos in Watts and Detroit in the 1960s. Too little is understood why some experience passivity, others antagonism, and still others a sense of personal mission to change the situation.

One other aspect merits attention. Themism probably reaches a peak when a person (1) recognizes the problem but (2) is unsure of the best answer for it and (3) has insufficient skill to involve others in the critique necessary for learning how to solve it. When conditions comparable with those above are present, training in skills of critique is probably the best single way to reduce resistance to change.

Increasing Observation Skills

There are a number of practical ways to assist participants in evaluating their personal accuracy in observation to increase the validity of their perceptions, and to test their own themism tendencies.

Videotapes and audiotapes offer a useful way of recording events as they occur. When reviewed after a participant has made verbal or written accounts of observations, it is possible to check the observations against the actual record of facts.

A second way is for participants to engage in an activity which, at some point in time, is interrupted. A selected person leaves the group and reconstructs the situation experience in a critique-based way, identifying sound features that should be continued or strengthened, and unsound features that should be reduced or eliminated. While the selected person is engaged in this reconstruction, other members make similar observations but interact with one another so as to put the pieces of a jigsaw puzzle together in a more complete and consensus-based way. The absent member now returns and describes the observations. The team tests the accuracy of what was observed against the consensus-based conclusions they had agreed on during the selected person's absence. Identified discrepancies can produce useful learning. The third step is for the group to prepare a critique of how the evaluated person can increase the accuracy of the observations.

Summary

A good climate for learning from critique has been described as depending upon explicit norms for creating an open sharing of agreement about the purposes to be achieved, creating and maintaining a problem-solving rather than a win/lose environment, inviting confrontational feedback, and making it legitimate to express feelings and emotions.

By making the best use of critique as part of their problem-solving and decision-making processes, organizations can gain several advantages. With critique, actions are likely to be sounder because they are taken only after reservations and doubts have been identified and answered or resolved. Members feel more involvement and commitment after critique because they have had a chance to understand and contribute. The side effects of proposed actions can be avoided through critique because they are more likely to be identified in advance or along the way.

By practicing critique in one situation, each member is more likely to be able to make effective use of it for learning in other situations, in other places, with other people.

SEVEN

Perspectives about Learning

Two basically different approaches to learning were mentioned in Chapter 1. One involves the school system, which aids people to learn and understand codified knowledge. By studying what has been learned by others, it becomes unnecessary for future generations to learn by starting afresh. This is the "time-binding" function of classroom education. Though the effectiveness of educational institutions in carrying out this function leaves much to be desired, learning from manuscripts is fundamental to an effective society.

Critique learning is the other major approach. Compared with learning subjects of the kind taught in the classroom, it involves the act of learning how to learn directly from work experience. The systematic approach of critique has only recently come into focus, yet its pertinence for solving many of the chronic problems that plague individuals and institutions is already quite evident.

Critique Methods Applied to the Work Structure

Direct experience as represented in the different structures of work represents the activities in which people engage on a daily basis.

How various methods can be employed for work improvement is shown in Table 2 and described in more detail below.

TABLE 2   How Critique Methods Relate to the Structure of Work

How is the work structured?	Discrete projects	Recurring activity cycles	Continuous flow
What are the preferred critique approaches?	Action research modeling; simulation, (model building, dry run, pilot projects); inspection, (commission, board of inquiry, debriefing); participation observation (post-mortem, process observers).	Ideal-actual research modeling, (zero-based budgeting); obligation models, (sunset laws, affirmative action programs); participant observation, (PMR, post-mortem); simulation.	Force field analysis; inspection; simulation, (model building); deviation analysis.

SOURCE: From *Seminar on Strategies of Critiques* Materials. Copyright © Scientific Methods, Inc., 1977.

Discrete projects

When each project is both unique and a complete unit of activity, the action research model, which begins with "pure" goal setting in the sense that there are no past practices to depart from, is ideally suited to this type of work. Once established, the goal serves to orient planning, and action steps follow from the plan. The data-gathering step allows study of (1) how well goals are being met, (2) whether they need to be modified in the light of operational realities, and (3) how anticipated future steps may need to be modified.

Simulation through model building also is an appropriate learning strategy in discrete project situations. Given a specifiable goal, it may be necessary to design a simulation model to grasp what might be required for achieving that goal. The NASA space program, particularly the moon shot, provided many examples of this. *Dry runs* and *pilot projects* also can provide preapplication learning pertinent for increasing project effectiveness.

Recurring activity cycles

The approach most useful with activity cycles when the goal to be achieved is not taken for granted is formulated by designing an actual-ideal model. This approach identifies, in the ideal, what should be, without intrusions from the past. The actual model specifies what is or has been true of cycles completed in the immediate past. Comparing these two provides a basis for understanding (1) what has been done in the past that should be continued, (2) what has been done in the past that should be discontinued, and (3) what should be done in the future that has not been done in the past. These three considerations lead to goal setting that relates the past to the future, and in this way it can help break up recurrent patterns. Begun by setting goals in this way, the steps in a classical Action Research Model may be followed in a more or less standard sequence.

Zero-based budgeting is another approach to cycle breaking. Rather than starting with an ideal-actual formulation, however, it proceeds from the opposite direction. The hypothesis is that *nothing* would be the ideal. This has to be disproved in order for something to be continued. The hypothesis forces an examination of each action in a previous cycle to determine what if anything it contributed. Since the ideal is nothing, then each feature of the actual situation is subjected to rigorous assessment as to whether the activity should be continued and, if so, whether it should be modified in some way. Participation observation is also useful in developing heightened awareness of change possibilities for strengthening activity cycle kinds of work.

Continuous flow

Force field analysis is one of the better ways of diagnosing the influences that hold the level in a continuous flow situation in its more or less steady state and that prevent it from shifting up or down. Once identified, goals can be set for shifting the level and plans developed for removing restraining forces or adding the driving forces necessary for bringing the change about.

Inspection techniques are also useful for spotting deviations from standard procedures in a continuous flow activity. Causes can be determined and action steps taken to rectify the situation at points where such deviations occur.

Simulation is another useful critique method for learning how to increase understanding of a continuous flow activity. The activity itself can continue in the routine manner, but at the same time various models can be designed and tested for alternative and more effective ways to achieve the desired continuous flow. If one mode of organization proves to be better than another, a shiftover from the actual activity to the requirements as specified by the model can take place.

Improved management and supervision can strengthen teamwork, but use of critique is the main link that permits people to solve problems to improve production. Without critique, an organization is likely to repeat its mistakes; with it, possibilities of progress are limitless. Yet progress in utilizing critique for learning has been far slower than progress in designing formal educational systems.

Barriers

There may be definite reasons beneath the surface for the reluctance to employ critique as a method of learning. Some possible barriers are discussed below.

Confusion between criticism and critique

Any method which examines what is occurring in a situation that needs evaluation can lead to such emotional reactions as feeling blamed or criticized. A widespread reaction to blame and criticism is the feeling of being attacked. When persons feel attacked, they are likely to respond with anger, hostility, and defensiveness. The risk in trying to gain the benefits obtainable from critique is that anger and hostility will be provoked, resulting in the situation worsening rather than improving. Because of this concern, benefits are often foregone to avoid negative results anticipated from anger and hostility.

Climate of noncollaboration

There are, of course, exceptions to the statements that follow, but many of the specific critique methods rely on collaboration or cooperation among those engaged in an experience. However, many of our most common operating situations are based on an authority/obedience relationship, such as between boss and subordinate, parent and child, doctor and patient, and so on. It is in the tradition of authority/obedience for the person in the supervised role to do whatever is instructed. It is not in this tradition for a boss to consult in a collaborative way. Often such collaboration only occurs when the boss does not know what to do and the only way to solve a problem is to seek a subordinate's participation in trying to understand its nature, extent, impact, and causes. Because of this tradition of noncollaboration in the planning, organizing, and directing aspects of the activities in which people engage, it is particularly difficult to shift the basis of relationship from hierarchical supervision to nonhierarchical consultation to get the most effective critique.

Another aspect of the barriers in a climate of noncollaboration is contained in many of our assumptions about individual responsibility. These assumptions are based on the notion that in the final analysis *individuals are responsible* for all that happens to them. Only they can explain why circumstances are as they are. The creation of conditions favorable to critique can thus sometimes raise doubts as to whether individual responsibilities are being sacrificed in the interest of learning.

Pressures for production

Many approaches to critique rely on a calm and unpressured environment. Only then are participants able to freely exchange ideas. Creating a relatively calm environment is not easy in circumstances where a premium is placed on getting immediate short-term results. There is no time to pause, consider, and discuss. This reaction hides a deeper feeling that over the long term more achievement will result from keeping people busy than can accrue from learning about increased effectiveness that discussion might produce. Sometimes the short-term payoff from keeping one's nose to the grindstone appears much more attractive than the possible anxiety raised by "thinking" and discussion.

Skills for critique

Another limitation is related to lack of skill in making effective use of critique. These skills are discussed in Chapter 6; they involve active listening; asking open-ended, nonjudgmental questions; giving personal feedback without arousing defensiveness; and so on. These are learnable skills but the barrier is in a reluctance to apply time and energy to acquiring them. The benefits that may or may not result from employing critique as the basis for introducing change might not, it is said, justify the effort.

Trying to introduce critique without anticipating and resolving the above barriers is only likely to increase resistance to its use. Open and frank identification, discussion, and impromptu feedback of these and related observations is the best approach. When thrashed through, they are likely to lose their importance. If they persist, there may be good reasons for them. By identifying these reasons, improved objectivity in introducing critique may be possible. A related aspect involves participation. Those who share a problem in common need to collaborate in its solution. All need to know critique methodologies and how to use them. Critique seminars are useful for this purpose.[1]

Benefits

Many potential benefits are available to individuals and institutions through the more effective use of critique for problem identification, learning about underlying causes, and studying corrective ways of bringing improvement to the situation. The benefits are discussed below.

More effective management

More intelligent management can be applied to a broader range of problems. It has been observed that many problems go unresolved because their existence is not recognized, or they are not seen as being solvable because there is no way to get people involved in applying their thinking to them. Critique can overcome this limitation, making it unnecessary to live with bad situations.

---

[1]Information regarding Seminars on Strategies of Critique is available from Scientific Methods, Inc., Box 195, Austin, Tex. 78767.

Better use of resources

It is a common observation that even though equipment and people may seem to be fully occupied, they have resources to contribute above and beyond what is currently asked of them. By increasing opportunities for making contributions, better use of resources can be made and greater satisfaction can be achieved by those who contribute. It follows, then, that more effective use of technology, finances, and so on becomes possible.

Seeing opportunities

When individuals share their perceptions of a problem, define it more clearly, and identify its causes and impacts, alternatives available for generating effective solutions become more clear. As a result, previously unseen opportunities may be recognized.

Higher performance standards

Critique can result in higher performance standards being set for what constitutes sound effort, because people come to value excellence when they contribute to its specification and achievement.

Heightened involvement

Critique can lead to a better understanding of what the true dynamics of the situation are. This, in turn, has the effect of increasing the total amount of control being exercised on problems by individuals themselves, without surveillance by higher levels in the organization.

Accelerating change

Critique accelerates change by penetrating the prison of traditions and past practices. It is a way of eliminating unsound precedents and the effects they bring about and of building on those that remain sound.

New knowledge

Better use can be made of the new knowledge available in various scientific and technological disciplines when those responsible for a situation are prepared to reject unsound existing knowledge and replace it with more up-to-date and valid information, methods, and concepts.

Learning to learn

What is learned from the repetitive use of critique can be systematized in ways that help people gain insight about the dynamics of personal and organizational achievement.

Implications of Critique for Improving Operational Effectiveness

The development of operational effectiveness in an organization—whether it is a commercial enterprise committed to profit, an educational institution committed to theoretical or vocational learning, or a hospital committed to patient care—rests first on the development of the individual. Then must come the development of the boss and subordinate teams which work together, followed by the intergroup teams which need to cooperate and coordinate their efforts. Finally, when individuals, work teams, and intergroups are working effectively as a whole, it becomes possible to begin organization development, that is, setting out the policies and strategies for the organization as a whole and for its growth, change, and development.

There is a range of approaches for developing an organization, but in one form or another all make use of critique methods of the sort described in this book. Organization development, however, involves additional elements for strengthening the processes of thinking and action that occur in an organization. Infusing an organization with theories more suitable to the accomplishment of results through people is one such element. Nonetheless, the introduction of new ideology is reinforced and buttressed by the use of critique to evaluate the effectiveness with which this is being accomplished. The use of critique enables organization members to translate theory into operational practices. Experience can be put to work through better use of critique.

The Critique Cube

As mentioned in Chapter 1, the concept of critique received impetus after World War II. Without a comprehensive framework useful for understanding its properties and uses, exploitation of these methodologies for work improvement has been rather slow. We therefore designed a framework through which to develop a systematic approach to this important source of learning from experience: The Critique Cube, shown in Figure 3, identifies the many possibilities for applying critique for work improvement.

The vertical axis shown on the left represents the four major techniques of critique: inspection, simulation, participant observation, and strategic assessment. The horizontal axis is along the bottom line. It shows the categories people use when evaluating any experience: product, performance, procedure, process, and people. Sometimes all can be seen. They are not different parts of an experience, but attributes from which a complex experience may be viewed.

The third dimension goes from the front to the back of the cube and is labeled on the right-hand margin. It identifies the formal categories we use to manage the work structures requiring the exercise and coordination of human effort, whether they are discrete projects, activity cycles, or continuous flow in nature. These categories are: planning, organizing, staffing, directing, and controlling. These are the actions to which insights acquired from critiquing a product, performance, or procedure can be applied to change or strengthen *future* behavior and performance as a result of critiquing and learning from *past* behavior and performance.

Some critique methods fit certain management functions better than others. For example, inspection is probably geared to problems of control, strategic assessment to planning, simulation to organizing, and participant observation to directing and staffing. Depending on the kind of evidence used for learning—product, performance, procedure, process, or people—it may be that other critique approaches or combinations of approaches are better suited for learning in specific situations.

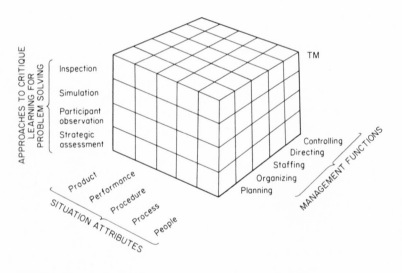

figure 3 *The Critique Cube.*

Index